The Edge of New Netherland

The Edge of New Netherland

Written and Illustrated
by

L. F. Tantillo

With a Historical Overview of the Delaware River
by
Charles T. Gehring
and
Commentary by Peter A. Douglas

Published for The New Netherland Institute

Cover illustration: Fort Casimir/Trinity, c. 1655 by L. F. Tantillo

Copyright @ 2011 by L.F. Tantillo
Published by L. F. Tantillo, Fine Art, Nassau, New York
Printed in the USA

Published in its initial form under special license to The New Netherland Institute.

Edited, designed and illustrated by Len Tantillo

ISBN:1461060958

Table of Contents

Preface

For most of my life I have been fascinated by the early history of the northeastern United States. This is in no small part due to the fact that I was born and raised here. Here, for me, was the little town of New Paltz, not far from the Hudson River in New York State. I grew up with a knowledge of the Dutch presence simply because so many stone houses of Dutch design from the 18th century had been preserved there. Who were these settlers? How did they get along with the Indians? How did they build their houses? What was colonial life like? The questions of my youth have expanded exponentially and still linger today.

Writing and illustrating this book about New Netherland, New Sweden, early North American fortification design, and the construction of Fort Casimir has provided me with an opportunity to study in detail an overlooked episode in 17th century history. Often unnoticed is that New Netherland, the colony established by the Dutch West India Company in 1621, encompassed more than the Hudson Valley of New York State. It extended far to the east, south, and west including most of Connecticut, New Jersey, part of Pennsylvania, and all of Delaware.

Fort Casimir is fascinating because it is so unremarkable. It was made of wood and dirt, was poorly maintained, failed every time it was tested in battle and rotted away to dust. Not much to marvel about, this is true. What makes Fort Casimir interesting is that it was typical of the simple fortifications built in New Netherland. Fort Orange in Albany and Fort Amsterdam in Manhattan were similar in general design and construction. The letters of Director General Petrus Stuyvesant state over and over again the dismal conditions of these facilities and the disastrous consequences that would inevitably occur if the colony were to come under attack.

How these inexpensive and expeditious forts were built and why so little attention was paid to maintaining them will be explored in this book. Along the way we will take a look at some of the reasons why Europeans were interested in colonizing North America, how beaver fur was obtained, traded, and processed, and the valuable items of exchange used in the barter system. We will also examine in detail how planked fort bastions may have been built. In concluding chapters we will study the rise and fall of Fort Casimir and the early history of New Castle, Delaware, as it emerged from the Dutch colony of New Amstel.

When I began this project I was already familiar with the New York forts, having spent many years studying and painting them. I did not, however, have any experience with Fort Casimir or Delaware River history. I thought it would be interesting to invite my friend and talented writer, Peter Douglas, to observe the process of researching and depicting these subjects. Using his formidable skills, Peter has documented his observations and provides readers with an insight into the developing ideas presented herein.

It is important to note from the start that this is one person's interpretation of historical information. I have worked long and hard at trying to understand how it all went together and, like all the others who have attempted this before me, there can be no absolute certainty that one's assumptions are correct. All I can say is, that with the facts as I know them now, this is the way the story unfolds.

L. F. Tantillo, 2011

A preliminary study of a New Netherland
sawmill, circa 1650

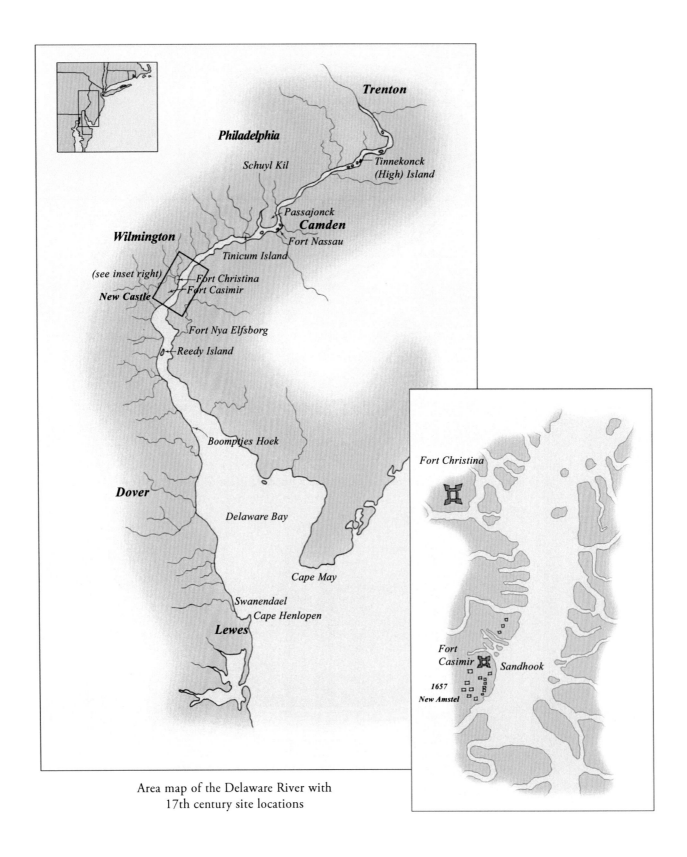

Area map of the Delaware River with
17th century site locations

"The Edge of New Netherland" is my attempt to explain and illustrate what was built in New Castle, Delaware in 1651, specifically Fort Casimir. In order to achieve a better understanding of the subject, I have depicted aspects of life in New Netherland, an explanation of 17th century fort construction, the details of Fort Casimir as well as renditions of the community it protected. Before delving into this material reading "De Suyt Rivier," by Charles T. Gehring will give the reader greater insight into the early history of Delaware and enhance the experience of discovery that follows. - Len Tantillo

De Suyt Rivier
New Netherland's Delaware Frontier

by Charles T. Gehring

The four hundred pound governor of New Sweden welcomed the crew of the Dutch ship and asked the skipper if he sailed often in this river. When the skipper answered no, the governor expressed surprise that he was able to come up this far in waters so full of sand bars. The Dutch skipper pointed to the man at his side and said that it was he who told him how to navigate the river. Whereupon one of the governor's officers stepped forward and said that he knew the man, as he himself had often been to Manhattan. He added that the man had been a patroon of Swanendael at the entrance of the bay that it had been destroyed by the Indians in 1630 when no Swedes even knew of this river.

The year was 1643. The Swedish governor was Johan Printz—veteran of the Thirty Years' War. The Dutch pilot was none other than David Pietersz de Vries—not only a former patroon of Swanendael near Cape Henlopen (Delaware) but also one of the most skillful sailors ever to come out of the Netherlands. It had been 34 years since Hudson had sailed into Delaware Bay and the waterway was still surrounded by mystery and danger.

The ship was a herring *buys* (buss) out of Rotterdam carrying one hundred pipes of Madeira wine. The skipper, Jacob Blenck, didn't have the slightest idea where he was. According to De Vries' journal, Blenck had been looking for Virginia to dispose of his cargo. Sailing by way of the West Indies Blenck had been unable to find the Chesapeake and had ended up in Boston. Unable to sell his cargo there because of the "sober lifestyle" of the English, he sailed on to Manhattan. Unfortunately the Dutch had just captured a ship full of wine, so Blenck was also unable to market his cargo there. However, an

Englishman at Manhattan finally bought the Madeira for delivery in Virginia. Blenck just had to find someone to pilot him to the Chesapeake since he had already missed the area once on his own. As unlucky as Blenck seems to have been up to this point he was fortunate to find David Pietersz de Vries as a pilot.

De Vries was nearing the end of his career, which he had pursued as supercargo and ship's master from the Mediterranean to the Far East. His adventurous career is recorded in travel journals, which he kept for most of his activities at sea. In 1630 he became an investor in Swanendael, a patroonship granted through the directors of the West India Company. Its location, at the southwestern entrance to Delaware Bay, was chosen for the establishment of a factory to process trane oil taken from the whales that frequented these waters. Twenty-eight men were sent over who immediately built a large brick trading house protected by a stockade. Unfortunately a misunderstanding over the punishment of an Indian accused of stealing a metal boundary marker led to the death of all but one of the settlers. De Vries first visited the New World shortly after word had been received of the disaster. He met with the Indians at Swanendael and struck an accord with them, becoming acquainted with their language in the process. Several other voyages to New Netherland made him one of the most knowledgeable navigators of North American waters.

The herring *buys* followed the coast of New Jersey until Delaware Bay. There De Vries recognized Cape May at the southern tip of New Jersey. He instructed Blenck to sail in on the south west side close by the shore near Cape Henlopen. As they approached the shoreline Blenck noted that he had been here over seven weeks ago; and had even gone ashore to ask directions of some natives he had spotted on the bank fishing. After attempts to communicate in Spanish failed, and because of the numerous sand bars, he had put out to sea again, ending up in Boston. Upon hearing this De Vries responded: "If you knew the Indian language as I do, you wouldn't have sailed to New England. This land is called Swanendael, and these Indians destroyed the beginnings of my colony in 1630. If you had been able to communicate with them, they would have brought you up the river to the Swedes or to our people who would have told you that you had sailed past Virginia."

Although the directors of the West India Company had at first considered this southern region of New Netherland the most suitable center of the colony, two decades later it remained *terra incognita* to many. Early explorations of the bay and river by Cornelis Hendricksz, Cornelis Jacobsz May and others apparently led to the conclusion that the climate was similar to that of Florida. Either they had never spent a winter on the upper reaches of the Delaware or had experienced a series of mild winter seasons, because, based on their reports, the directors initially had selected High Island (now Burlington Island) as the administrative center of New Netherland. This all soon changed because of events far to the north.

When Peter Minuit arrived in the colony in the spring of 1626 to replace Willem Verhulst as director, he was faced with an unexpected problem with far-reaching ramifications. Contrary to instructions, Daniel van Crieckenbeeck, the local commander at Fort Orange on the upper Hudson, had taken sides in the struggle between the Mahicans and Mohawks for control of the west bank of the river. While marching off with a Mahican war party to attack the Mohawks, they were ambushed several miles from the fort. Crieckenbeeck and three of the six soldiers with him were killed. The Mohawks were not pleased that the Dutch had decided to support their ancestral enemy. Although Minuit rushed to Fort Orange and managed to stabilize the situation, the safety of the outlying settlements was now questionable at best. Minuit responded by consolidating the agricultural support families on Manhattan, which he had purchased shortly after his arrival. Not only were the families at Fort Orange resettled in the more secure environment of lower Manhattan, but also those families that had been settled at the Connecticut River, and on High Island in the Delaware.

Minuit's decisive actions were not mere knee-jerk reactions of a green commander under pressure. He knew exactly what he was doing. This was his second tour of duty in New Netherland. Before returning to patria in 1625 he had served under Verhulst as a volunteer. In this capacity he was instructed to travel from one end of the colony to the other, reporting on the condition and resources of the land. This knowledge of the geographical configuration of New Netherland, especially the South river region, would serve him well in his later years. In order to manage New Netherland effectively it was necessary to have a thorough understanding of its major waterways. A glance at a map shows that the colony was oriented along two axes, the North and South rivers. It was important to understand that the South River found its origins not far to the west of Fort Orange. It soon became clear that whoever controlled access to the Delaware Valley and its upper reaches could also control or at least threaten the fur trading operation at Fort Orange. The Dutch already knew about this crucial geographical fact as early as 1615.

Operating out of Fort Nassau on Castle Island (now part of the port of Albany), a man named Kleyntie and two companions headed west into Iroquois country; probably following the Normanskill. Near the headwaters of the Delaware river they were captured by the Minquaes Indians (or Susquahannocks, an Iroquoian speaking people not in the confederacy). The following year, Cornelis Hendricksz learned of their captivity while trading in the South river and arranged to have them ransomed. Kleyntie's wanderings, both as explorer and captive, added valuable information to the cartographic knowledge of the colony, and revealed the proximity of New Netherland's two major river systems.

As important as the South river was strategically the WIC simply did not have the resources to devote to the region. It became clear early on that Fort Orange would be the major trading post in the colony. In fact, Fort Nassau (present-day Gloucester, NJ) that replaced the abandoned trading operation on High Island could not be manned on a regular basis. During the winter of 1633 De Vries approached Fort Nassau looking for food only to find it occupied by Indians. Although the Dutch were unable to defend against encroachment by other trading powers, the treacherous entrance to the bay and the hostility of the Indians proved to be their best ally. When De Vries offered to trade with the Indians at Fort Nassau for beans, they told him to bring his ship to anchor in a nearby narrow stream. Only an Indian woman who spoke Dutch saved them from certain ambush. De Vries later learned that nine Englishmen had been killed by a similar ploy in the preceding year. [By the way, De Vries rewarded the woman with a cloth dress.] For over a decade the South river, although neglected by the Dutch, remained accessible only to an experienced few such as De Vries and Minuit. Although the former had a persistent interest in this southern region since his ill-fated Swanendael, it would be the latter who would force the WIC to reconsider its priorities.

In 1635 De Vries was at Manhattan when a Dutch ship returned from the South river with fifteen Englishmen. They had been sent up from the English at Point Comfort in Virginia to occupy the Dutch fort in the Delaware. When the director of New Netherland, Wouter van Twiller, learned of this, he sent a force down to remove the interlopers. Although De Vries had other business and other plans, Van Twiller persuaded him to take the Englishmen back to Virginia. When he entered the harbor another ship with twenty soldiers was about to leave for Fort Nassau as a reinforcement. Upon learning of the fate of the previous party the mission was aborted. The proximity of the English at Virginia and Maryland would seem to make them the logical competitor of the Dutch in the Delaware Valley. A base of operations in the valley would have made it possible for the English to move up the valley west of the Hudson, threatening the Dutch trading alliance with the Mohawk and with the potentiality of splitting the patroonship of Rensselaerswijck from the rest of the colony. This was a fear actually expressed by Petrus Stuyvesant in 1649. Although the Dutch had been aware of the geographical dimensions of their colony since Kleyntie's adventure in 1615, the English in the tobacco colonies were not quite sure what lay beyond the Chesapeake. However, not only were the English ignorant of the geographical possibilities in this region, they would have been hard pressed to make any move into Iroquois country on the upper Delaware. The vulnerability of the southern frontier, especially from probes out of the Chesapeake, would be demonstrated several times throughout the history of New Netherland. However, it would be the Swedes who would gain a foothold in the Delaware, forcing the Dutch to focus more resources on this neglected region. In 1632 Peter Minuit was on his way back to the Netherlands. Charges of mismanagement (mostly unfounded) led to his discharge from the Company's service. Minuit did not remain unemployed for long. His knowledge acquired while director of New Netherland made him an attractive candidate to investors looking for someone to direct a new trading operation in North America. Although the New Sweden Company was chartered by the Swedish government much of its financial resources came from the Netherlands. One of them was Samuel Blommaert an investor along with David Pietersz de Vries in the ill-fated patroonship of Swanendael. Minuit arrived in the Delaware in 1638 with two ships carrying materials and equipment to establish a trading colony. After negotiating with the natives for land on the Minquaes Kil (now Christina Creek in Wilmington, Delaware), he built a fort and began his trading operation . Minuit's knowledge of the region placed the fort on the west side of the river at the mouth of a waterway frequented by natives coming in from the west. The Dutch trading operation at Fort Nassau on the east side of the river had suddenly become an anachronism. The Swedes at Fort Christina (named after the Swedish queen) were also in a position to monitor and potentially impede Dutch river traffic to their post, located farther to the north. Although the West India Company's jurisdiction on the South River had been violated, the Dutch at Manhattan did not react to the presence of the Swedes in the same manner as they had when the English had occupied Fort Nassau several years before.

As luck would have it a new director had just been installed in New Netherland. Willem Kieft, Van Twiller's replacement, issued a formal protest, which Minuit ignored. Kieft attempted no military action against the Swedes. As a new director with no previous experience in the area (unlike Minuit) he probably was unsure of his options and the international ramifications of doing violence to the colony of a friendly European power. So he hesitated; probably awaiting instructions from the directors in Amsterdam. In any case Kieft soon became involved in a protracted war with the natives around Manhattan, leaving him with few resources to devote to the South River. Rather than an attitude of confrontation Kieft developed one of accommodation with New Sweden.

Accommodation soon turned into cooperation when in 1641 a boat load of English settlers from New Haven arrived in the South River to start a settlement in the Schuyl Kil (now Philadelphia). The Swedes and the Dutch teamed up to thwart this incursion by returning the settlers to New Haven aboard a Dutch ship and by burning their buildings. Both Kieft and the Swedes at Fort Christina realized that the significant danger at this time was English expansion and not one another.

As New Sweden received new colonists and supplies from the home country, expanding its area of influence, friction between the two European traders in the Delaware grew. In 1645 a new commander at Fort Nassau ended the era of accommodation with the Swedes. Andries Hudde instituted a more aggressive policy of protecting the Company's jurisdiction and trading interests in the South River. Although the Dutch trading post at Fort Nassau was on the "wrong" side of the river, Hudde had one major advantage over his adversary, Johan Printz (governor of New Sweden): a consistent supply of trade goods. Swedish supply ships came at sporadic intervals, often leaving the colonists to their own devices for long periods of time. Once during Printz' governorship not a single relief ship reached the colony for over six years. The natives hated nothing more than to struggle through the wilderness with heavy packs of furs only to find that the European traders had nothing to offer. A trip across the river to the Dutch at Fort Nassau then became less of an annoyance. Printz countered the Dutch advantage by employing methods to hinder Dutch relations with the natives such as spreading rumors of Dutch plans to exterminate the natives, and destruction of Dutch buildings on the west bank of the river along the Schuyl Kil. His draconian tactics kept the Dutch off balance until the arrival of Petrus Stuyvesant as director general of New Netherland in 1648.

Stuyvesant could be just as aggressive and intimidating as Printz. After a series of maneuverings in the Schuyl Kil to establish a trading post called Beversreede, Stuyvesant shifted his focus. For two years he was unable to deal forcefully with the Swedes because of continued threats from New Haven to form a colony in the South River. Stuyvesant knew, as stated earlier, that if the English were allowed to settle there the entire colony would be threatened from behind. Although there was friction between the Dutch and Swedes they needed to cooperate in order to keep the English out. This all changed in 1650 with the signing of the Treaty of Hartford. Although the major points of agreement concerned the settlement of conflicting boundary claims between New England and New Netherland, one of the matters resolved at the conference concerned New Haven's attempts to settle in the South River. The agreement stated that any future attempt would not have the approval of the other colonies of New England, and that New Haven would be left to its own devices if trouble should arise as a result. Now that it seemed that the New Haven distraction had been resolved, Stuyvesant was ready to deal with the Swedes in a more decisive manner.

Without any apparent instructions from his superiors in Amsterdam, Stuyvesant led an impressive military force into the Delaware Valley. Over one hundred soldiers marching overland from Manhattan, linked up with a fleet of eleven ships that had sailed upriver to Fort Nassau with drums beating on their decks. With such a formidable force Stuyvesant could have eliminated the Swedish colony then and there; however, he was acting on his own initiative and probably did not want to chance an international incident. In any case his plans at this time involved strategic maneuvering rather than war. When his naval and ground forces assembled at Fort Nassau (approximately opposite the mouth of the Schuyl Kil) he proceeded to dismantle the fort and transport whatever was moveable to a new site on the west side of the river. The new location was known as Sant Hoeck by the Dutch (now the site of New Castle, Delaware). It had a deep harbor, access to trade routes to the west, and commanded the river. Not only did the Dutch now have a trading post on the "right" side of the river for the Indian trade, but its location south of Fort Christina gave the Dutch the ability to monitor and control river traffic. Stuyvesant named his new stronghold Fort Casimir in memory of Ernst Casimir of the house of Orange-Nassau, a hero of his native province of Friesland. The directors were upset that he had demolished Fort Nassau without their approval; they were also puzzled by his reasons for the name of the new installation. They admonished him to guard the new fort well, and to give the Swedes no further cause for complaint, as they needed no more enemies. The first Anglo-Dutch war was about to begin.

You can imagine Stuyvesant's embarrassment, let alone anger, when Fort Casimir was surrendered to the Swedes without firing a shot. This time Johan Printz was not involved. He had become so discouraged with the situation in New Sweden that he decided to take his family back to Sweden. It had been five years since he had received a relief ship. He had been governor for ten years and there seemed little prospect for improvement. If he was to be replaced, he would have to initiate it himself. So in 1653 he trekked overland to Manhattan and caught the first ship to the Netherlands. Left in command of the Swedish colony was Printz' son-in-law Johan Papegoja. Shortly after setting sail for home, Printz' replacement and 200 colonists left Sweden for the Delaware Valley. They may very well have passed one another at sea. The Swedish relief consisted of two ships: *Örn* ("The Eagle") carrying the new governor Johan Rising and the colonists directly to the Delaware;

and *Gyllene Hay* ("The Golden Shark") carrying the new commissary Hendrick von Elswick. Before continuing on to New Sweden, Von Elswick was to proceed first to Puerto Rico where he was instructed to settle matters concerning the Swedish relief ship *Kattan* ("The Cat"), which had wrecked off its coast and was plundered by the Spaniards in 1649.

Rising's instructions were to attempt to remove the Dutch from Fort Casimir by argument and protest but to show no hostility. If unsuccessful he was to tolerate the Dutch there and build a fort below them to render Casimir ineffective. It was important that the fort should not fall into English hands during the Anglo-Dutch war, as they were "the strongest and consequently the most dangerous." After a stormy crossing Rising anchored before Fort Casimir on May 21ˢᵗ, 1654 (Julian calendar)—Trinity Sunday. With a ship full of over 200 people and a good verbal bluff Rising was able to effect the surrender of Fort Casimir without firing a shot. Rising renamed the post *Fort Trefaldighet* (Fort Trinity) in honor of the day on which it was taken. Because of the war with England and the threat of an invasion from the New England colonies, the South River had been stripped of most of its armaments to defend Manhattan. During this unsettling period of war with England, Stuyvesant's least concern was with New Sweden. The Company's reservations about dismantling Fort Nassau had been borne out. The Dutch were now left with no strongholds on the South River. News of the loss of the South River must have put a damper on the festivities celebrating the end of the war with England. Stuyvesant must have been furious. However, fate soon tempered his rage.

Remember Hendrick von Elswick and the "Golden Shark"? On his way north from Puerto Rico he missed the entrance to Delaware Bay. Unlike Jacob Blenck he did not end up in Boston, rather he sailed smartly in behind Staten Island where his ship was soon detected and confiscated. Von Elswick's protests were in vain; Stuyvesant stated that the ship, crew, and cargo would be restored as soon as Fort Casimir was returned to its rightful owners. Von Elswick eventually made his way overland to New Sweden, leaving behind the "Golden Shark" and most of the crew and passengers, who apparently decided to stay in New Amsterdam. Von Elswick had not seen the last of Stuyvesant. Although Johan Rising, the new governor of the Swedish colony, had lost a ship, he had gained an entire river; however, forces were already at work that would soon deprive him of everything.

Peace with England had given the directors in Amsterdam the opening to deal severely with the Swedes. They instructed Stuyvesant to do his "utmost to revenge this misfortune not only by restoring matters to their former condition, but also by driving the Swedes at the same time from the river, as they did us." They urged Stuyvesant to carry out the expedition before the Swedes could be reinforced and promised him military support; the directors reminded him that he could use his troops on Manhattan more freely now that there was peace with England. Stuyvesant assembled a force of over three hundred soldiers, divided into five companies. With a fleet of seven ships, including *De Waegh*, a large warship on loan from the city of Amsterdam, the invasion force set sail from Manhattan on Sunday, the 5th of September, after divine service. Stuyvesant bluffed his way past the guns of *Fort Trefaldighet*, landing troops just to the north. This maneuver cut off communications between Fort Christina and the former Dutch fort. The latter surrendered without firing a shot. When news reached Rising at Fort Christina of the situation to the south, he sent Hendrick von Elswick down to learn of Stuyvesant's intentions. When the Dutch commander made clear that he intended to take the entire river, the Swede retorted: "*Hodie mihi, cras tibi*" (Today me, tomorrow you). Stuyvesant passed the remark off as an idle threat but, as we know, Von Elswick's words proved to be prophetic. Stuyvesant moved his forces north to Fort Christina with the intention of reducing it if Rising refused to surrender. Outgunned and surrounded the governor of New Sweden signed terms of capitulation on the 25th of September. The entire river had been returned to the Dutch. The Swedes protested strongly, stating that the Dutch claim to the river as right of first discovery by Hudson in 1609 did not hold. Otherwise it would belong to the Spanish or English. They argued that "discovered" land had to be occupied quickly after purchase or it reverted to the native owners. They countered the Dutch claim that they had built three trading houses from the falls to the mouth of the bay by pointing out that the house on High Island and Fort Nassau had been abandoned; and the colony of Swanendael was not sealed with their blood, as the Dutch claimed, but rather with their lives they also lost their rights. They contended that Fort Casimir was built on land purchased by the Swedes and had been so marked by poles carrying the insignia of the Crown; and that the fort had been founded with force and violence against firm protests, citing the rule of law: *quodquie, quid in aedificatur fundo, fundo cedit*, "That which is built upon the land, belongs to the owner of the land." Then they make the interesting argument that since the Dutch had been fearing an attack by the English, it was up to the Swedes to keep the fort from falling into English hands, citing: *aut nunc aut numquam*, "now or never." However, in the end the Dutch had the best argument of all: *beati possidentes*, "blessed are those who possess," or as the saying goes, "possession is nine points of the law."

If anything, the struggle with the Swedish colony forced the Dutch administration on Manhattan and the directors in Amsterdam to reconsider their plans for the South

River. It was no longer enough to visit the region occasionally for trading purposes, or to maintain a trading post only on a seasonal basis. The region had to be settled, as was happening in the Hudson Valley or it would be lost as had happened in the Connecticut Valley. The expedition against the Swedes not only stimulated interest in the region but also brought new players onto the stage. A major component of Stuyvesant's invasion force was the 36 gun warship *De Waegh*, "The Scales" or "Balance," carrying 200 men. Stuyvesant used the ship to great effect in the river; however, it was only on loan from the city of Amsterdam. Rather than pay for use of the ship and the 200 men brought over on it, the West India Company cleared its debt by granting the city all the land on the west side of the river from Christina Kill to Boompties Hoeck (now Bombay Hook, near Smyrna, Delaware). The city's territory became a colony within a colony called *Nieuwer Amstel*. The West India Company retained control over the land north of Christina Kil, including Fort Christina, renamed by the Dutch Fort Altena. The land south of Boompties Hoeck to Cape Henlopen also was retained by the Company. In 1663 the entire South River was given over to the administration of the city of Amsterdam. As the city's colony began to prosper and attract colonists in large numbers, it also drew the attention of the English in the tobacco colonies, especially Maryland.

After New Amstel had been visited by Nathaniel Utie, a local commander at the mouth of the Susquehanna River, and a troop of tobacco farmers, who threatened violence if the settlers on the South River refused to submit to English rule, Stuyvesant sent a diplomatic team to Maryland. Augustine Herrman and Resolved Waldron argued the Dutch position before the governor and council of Maryland on several occasions. The debate grew quite heated as one side countered the other's arguments. Herrman and Waldron had done their homework well. When the English claimed right of first discovery by Sir Walter Raleigh, they countered that they took their beginning from the king of Spain. When the English pointed out that the Dutch were not then an independent people, Hermans explained that they were vassals of the king when the discovery was made; and when the Dutch gained their freedom, the king conveyed full title to all his lands conquered by them. Tempers flared to such a point during this dinner discussion that the subject had to be changed. Several days later Governor Fendall let the Dutch emissaries examine Lord Baltimore's charter while he and his council were absent at another plantation. While taking notes and making extracts for use in further discussion, they found in the preamble that Baltimore's land area was limited by the phrase *hactenus inculta* (hitherto uncultivated). Herrman immediately used this discovery in further arguments with the governor, indicating that the Dutch had settled at Swanendael two years before Lord Baltimore had received his charter. Although no agreement was signed as a result of these discussions, the English were apparently impressed by the presentation of the Dutch claims. They came to realize that it would not be a simple matter of running the Dutch out of the Delaware by threats and intimidation. Much of these same arguments would be used by William Penn to defeat Maryland's claim to his three lower counties, which eventually became the colony of Delaware.

In conclusion, it may be of interest to know what happened to David Pietersz de Vries and Pieter Minuit. De Vries safely piloted the cargo of Madeira wine to Virginia. He visited in the Chesapeake area until the following year when he returned to his hometown of Hoorn in the Netherlands, never to go to sea again. Minuit set sail for Sweden with the *Kalmar Nyckel* a few months after establishing his colony on the Minquaes Kil. At the island of St. Christopher (now St. Kitts) in the Caribbean he traded wine and other goods for a cargo of tobacco. While waiting for his ship to be loaded he was invited aboard the Dutch ship *De Vliegende Hert* ("The Flying Deer"). A sudden hurricane blew the ship out to sea; Minuit was never seen again. Lying in the shadow of the Hudson River the often neglected South River has a colorful and sometimes tragic story to tell.

This article by Charles T. Gehring, "De Suyt Rivier: New Netherland's Delaware Frontier," was originally published by *de Halve Maen*, Journal of the Holland Society of New York, Summer 1992, Vol. LXV, Number 2: 21-25

"New Netherland is a very beautiful, pleasant, healthy and delightful land, where all manner of men can more easily earn a good living and make their way in the world than in the Netherlands or any other part of the globe that I know."

Adriaen van der Donck, 1655

Excerpt from "A Description of New Netherland" by Adriaen van der Donck, written in 1655 and 1656, edited by Charles T. Gehring and William A. Starna and translated by Diederik Willem Goedhuys.

1.

New Netherland

Thousands of pages of books, manuscripts, historical papers, and period documents have been devoted to the history of New Netherland. In terms of American history New Netherland's existence was short lived. Its impact on the developing nation that grew up in its wake was substantial. This section provides a brief pictorial overview of the 17th century Dutch Colony in North America.

New Netherland

A Pleasant and Healthy Land

During the 17th century a small European Protestant country comprised of seven provinces and ruled by a prince rather than a king, became a dominant international sea power and a leader in global trade. It is referred to as Holland, although Holland was only part of the country, The United Provinces of the Netherlands achieved a level of success unparalleled by a nation of its size in the colonial era.

In the New World the story began when an Englishman commanding a Dutch ship sailed into a great North American river. Henry Hudson's 1609 voyage in the *Halve Maen* ("Half Moon") set the stage for the development of the colony of New Netherland, in what is now the northeastern United States. New Netherland's existence was brief, lasting only fifty-five years. Its impact, however, was to ripple through American history for decades.

In 1621, the Geoctroyeerde Westindische Compagnie (GWC) was established. Translated, GWC is the Dutch West India Company. It was formed to regulate the emerging Atlantic trade. GWC administered newly discovered and potentially profitable jurisdictions in North and South America and the Caribbean. This area included New Netherland, which encompassed much of New York, Connecticut, New Jersey, Delaware, and part of Pennsylvania. This colony also possessed a unique river system and a magnificent protected island harbor. The primary rivers were the Hudson, the Connecticut, and the Delaware, which they called respectively the North, the Fresh, and the South Rivers. The island with the protected harbor was Manhattan.

Note: In this book GWC is used as the abbreviation for the Dutch West India Company because those are the letters which appear on the Company's flag. The more commom abbreviation is WIC.

Map of the northeastern United States. Present day state boundaries have been added for reference purposes.

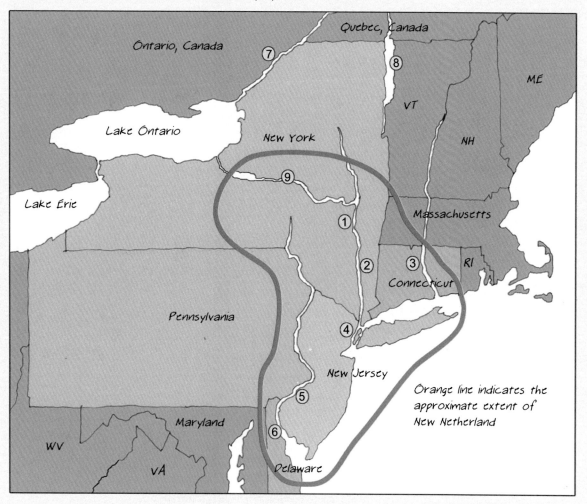

Orange line indicates the approximate extent of New Netherland

Flag of the Dutch West India Company

The flag of the Dutch West India Company is actuallly the state flag of the Netherlands with a logo superimposed in the center. The company name in Dutch is Geoctroyeerde Westindische Compagnie, hence the "GWC."

The map above represents the approximate bounds and limits of influence of New Netherland in the early to mid 17th century. English and Swedish claims and intrusions caused the boundaries to vary over time.

Map Key:
1. Fort Orange, (Albany, New York)
2. The Hudson River
3. The Connecticut River
4. Manhattan
5. The Delaware River
6. Fort Casimir, (New Castle, Delaware)
7. The Saint Lawrence River
8. Lake Champlain
9. Mohawk River

The Fur Trade
Trappers and Hunters

European relations with the native people of North America is a complex topic requiring far more attention than the scope of this book. Dozens of tribes, speaking various languages and following vastly different cultural practices, interacted with the Dutch across New Netherland. As a testament to their trading skill, the Dutch were able to communicate with them all and, with varying degrees of success, negotiate lucrative business agreements.

Initially it was fur in North America that interested Europeans. Native people knew where and how to obtain it. Conversely, Indians soon realized the value of iron tools, cloth, firearms, and all the other wonders of modern life presented to them by their unusual visitors. From the start of interaction between the two groups, beaver emerged as the commodity of exchange.

There were a number of ways native hunters caught the beaver. Traps, snares, arrows, and spears were all effective. There are even accounts of Indians destroying beaver lodges to take their prey. It seems doubtful that this practice was in widespread use since it would destroy essential animal habitat.

The most likely technique for taking fur-bearing animals was the deadfall trap. It could easily be assembled using a heavy object such as a rock or a log, propped up with a delicately fashioned trigger mechanism fashioned from three sticks. An animal was attracted to bait attached to the trigger. The slightest movement brought the stone down upon the prey. It was effective and simple. The animal was removed and the trap was reset. The successful trapper returned home rewarded with food and trading currency.

Tribal women processed the fur. First the hide was stretched out on a circular wooden frame made from sapling branches and rawhide cords. The inside skin was scraped clean of meat and fat and then smeared with a mixture of cooked brains or liver. After one to three days, the skin was washed and rubbed with a tight rope until it was dry and soft. When the trading party was ready, bundled furs were carried to forts and farmsteads where trade negotiations took place.

Beaver hides were prepared by the women of the tribe. After skinning the animal the pelt was stretched on a wooden hoop, scraped clean and then rubbed with cooked brains or liver and then dried.

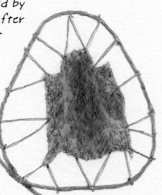

The Common Snare Trap

There are many variations of the common snare trap. They all work in basically the same way. An animal walks into a noose releasing a trigger that springs a bent sapling upward.

The deadfall trap is supported by the baited trigger mechanism.

The deadfall trap could be made from any heavy object like a rock or log propped up with an intricate trigger mechanism supporting one end of it. The weight of the heavy object needed to be many times the weight of the animal that was being caught.

The beaver is the largest rodent in North America and the third largest rodent in the world. Adults weigh from 30 to 80 pounds. A few have been known to weigh as much as 100 pounds. They can remain underwater for up to 15 minutes.

The North American Beaver
(Castor canadensis)

The Fur Trade
Bartering for Goods

The primary reason for building forts and establishing settlements in 17th-century North America was the fur trade. Beaver pelts brought high prices in Europe for the manufacturing of hats. The experienced Dutch were already expert global traders when Henry Hudson sailed into what is now New York State in 1609. It didn't take long for those skills to be applied to the subtle techniques of commercial interaction with Native Americans. Tribal languages and cultures varied greatly from one locale to another, yet the entrepreneurial Dutch quickly adapted. Traders found common ground, relying on products from Europe. Firearms, ammunition, gunpowder, iron tools, metal cooking utensils, cloth, pipes, and tobacco were some of the prized goods offered in exchange for fur. Additionally, and controversially, alcohol also made its way into Indian life.

Archeologists have often noted that some of the objects obtained in trade were transformed by Indian artisans to meet different requirements from those for which they were initially intended. For instance, an axe could be broken apart and re-ground to make specialized knives and scrappers. A copper kettle, instead of heating water, might be divided into smaller pieces and incorporated into jewelry or some other ornamental use. It mattered little to the trader as long as both parties felt satisfied with their barter agreement.

In addition to items of utility there was wampum or sewant, the beads made from the meticulous grinding and polishing of fragments of clamshells. These delicately shaped beads varied in value depending on their color and quality. An astute businessman soon learned to distinguish the difference. Wampum was like money in that it was accepted as currency among different tribes. For example, the Dutch might trade European goods with the Pequots along the Connecticut River and then use the Pequot wampum they had received to buy fur from the Mohawks.

The fundamental desire to engage in the transaction of mutually beneficial business superseded language and culture.

The iron trade axe was designed and manufactured to appeal to Native Americans, both in style and utility.

Bartering with guns was a dangerous business and from time to time when hostilities seemed inevitable the practice was banned.

Musket with a snaphaunce lock

Native Americans made wampum from shells. The quahog shell has variegated striations of color from a light ivory to a rich dark purple. Purple wampum was the most highly prized. Shells were broken up and the fragments were then carefully filed into shape and drilled lengthwise to make beads.

A string of purple and white wampum beads. To Dutch traders wampum was called sewant.

Hat Making
The Processing of Beaver Fur

The manufacturing of hats from beaver fur was big business. So much so, that by the early decades of the 17th century the beaver was nearly extinct in Europe. Perfect timing for the colonial development of New Netherland.

Acquiring furs from the Indians began the long and complex process of making a felt hat. Actual production began soon after the bundled pelts were delivered. The seemingly simple act of shipping, however, could be a long and tedious process. Ownership of the goods would sometimes change along the way delaying shipment. Once the haggling over prices and amassing of enough goods for commercially viable transport was concluded, the fur was loaded into the holds of Dutch merchant vessels and shipped to eager European manufacturers.

In the hands of skilled craftsmen, the best pelts were cleaned and then beaten with a bow, similar to that used with a violin. The course hairs were painstakingly plucked, one at a time by hand, leaving the softer innermost hairs, referred to as "beaver wool." The next step was called "fluffing." This entailed beating, heating, and steaming the fur and then treating it with a solution of nitrate of mercury. The mercury treatment caused two things to occur. The fiber pulled away from the hair shafts and facilitated the beginning of the felting process and the mercury poisoned most of the workers processing the fur. "Mad Hatter's Disease" was no joke.

After "fluffing," the resulting felt "batt" was rolled into a thin rectangular sheet and meticulously folded into a triangular shape. The resulting cone with an attached brim was then stretched over a wooden form to create the desired hat shape. The blocked hat was then dried, shaved, sanded, and lacquered or waterproofed. Trimming and lining finished the process. Hats of this type were made for men and women, although most beaver hats of the 17th century were made for men.

An interesting alternative to "hand plucking" was sometimes employed by the clever Dutch. The furs were shipped directly to Russia and made into coats. After a period of use the course outer hairs of the beaver pelt would simply wear off. At that point the old unwanted coats were bought back, shipped to the Netherlands and processed into felt, saving hours of hand labor.

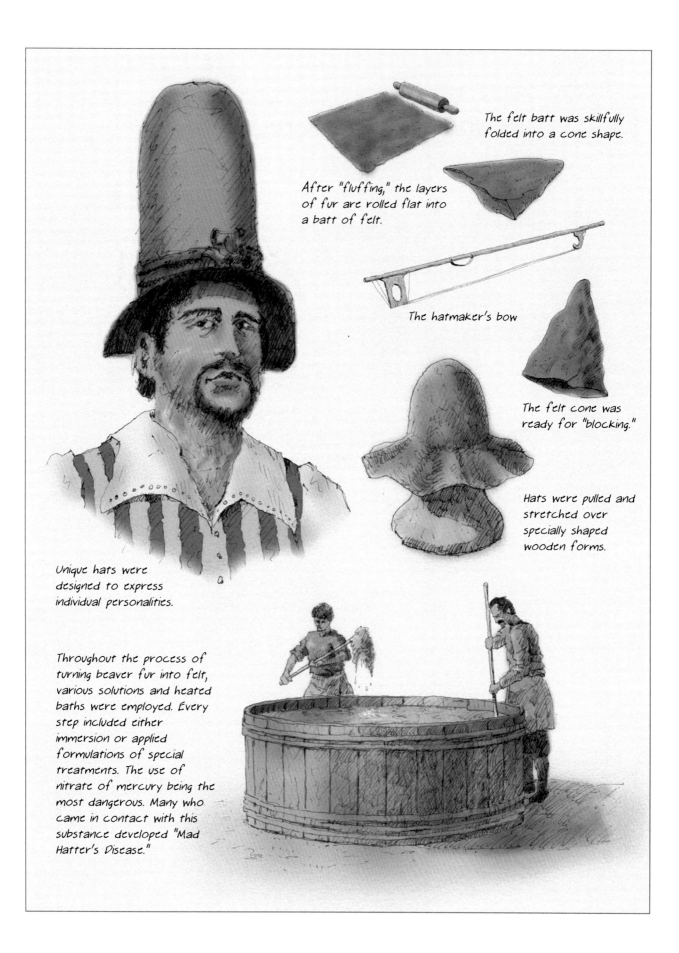

The felt batt was skillfully folded into a cone shape.

After "fluffing," the layers of fur are rolled flat into a batt of felt.

The hatmaker's bow

The felt cone was ready for "blocking."

Hats were pulled and stretched over specially shaped wooden forms.

Unique hats were designed to express individual personalities.

Throughout the process of turning beaver fur into felt, various solutions and heated baths were employed. Every step included either immersion or applied formulations of special treatments. The use of nitrate of mercury being the most dangerous. Many who came in contact with this substance developed "Mad Hatter's Disease."

The Business of New Netherland
Cash Crops and World Trade

New Netherland was established as a fur trading colony. The fur of the beaver was the most valuable. The purchase price from the Indians was 7 or 8 guilders per hide depending on quality. The pelt was resold for 10 or 12 guilders, with the price escalating each time the merchandise changed hands. Other valuable furs were otter, lynx, black bear, wolf, mountain lion, and elk. All of these selling for a little more than 4 guilders per hide. The lesser furs were bobcat, muskrat, mink, fox, fisher, and deer. These items usually sold for a guilder or less. The Indians also sold mats and baskets. Either item, depending on the level of craftsmanship, could cost as much as 6 guilders. Obviously the Indians did not accept guilders as payment. The exchange currencies were barter goods or wampum, referred to by the Dutch as sewant. In wampum 8 white beads or 4 purple beads equaled 1 stuiver. 24 stuivers equaled 1 guilder.

Trading for beaver furs was profitable and, without a doubt, the most well-known commercial enterprise in colonial North America. However, the economy driving the settlement of the New World was far more complex than a single commodity and, as years passed, beaver fur did not remain at the top of the list. English-controlled tobacco plantations shipped 1,500,000 pounds of tobacco in 1640. In 1690, it was 20,000,000 pounds. In Dutch currency that is 200,000 guilders in 1640, and 26,000,000 guilders in 1690, approximately 100 million dollars in today's currency. Tobacco was often traded directly from Virginia farmers to Dutch merchants to avoid the British tax of 2 shillings (about 2 guilders) per hogshead of tobacco. (1 hogshead equals 900 to 1,000 lbs.)

The prices for trade items of all sorts are clearly listed in Per Lindeström's "Geographia Americae," and in the "New York Historical Manuscripts: Dutch, volumes XVIII – XIX, Delaware Papers," translated by Charles T. Gehring.

Trading in agricultural products also contributed to the economic success of the Dutch West India Company. Wheat, barley, and other grains, along with alcohol, sugar, and dried fruits imported from other GWC colonies, exchanged hands in Manhattan for export to Europe. Domestically, it was native grown corn that rose to the top of the company's produce export market.

A hogshead was a large barrel measuring 30" in diameter at the top and bottom, and standing 48" tall. The word was derived from the Dutch "oxhooft." A hogshead of tobacco weighed from 900 to 1000 pounds.

Valuation of Colonial Currency:

Dutch   1 guilder = 24 stuivers
              1 lion daalder = 48 stuivers

English   1 pound = 240 pence
              1 shilling = 12 pence

Conversions:
     24 guilders = 1 pound
     8 white or 4 purple wampum beads = 1 stuiver

The Dutch referred to guilders or gulden as "florin," a name derived from an ancient coin struck in 1252 in Florence, Italy.

Lion symbol visible on the face of the coin below

A 1640 Dutch lion "daalder" silver coin was worth 48 stuivers. "Daalder" was later corrupted into the English word "dollar."

The Importance of the Delaware River
An Essential Component of the Trading Network

New Netherland may have been underfunded and lacked the attention paid to other Dutch colonial enterprises, but it was well organized. The Dutch West India Company understood the geography of their American colony. They realized early on the importance of the inland waterways and the potential of Manhattan as a centralized shipping port. The concept was simple. Manhattan was the hub. The Hudson, Delaware, and Connecticut Rivers provided access routes to interior trading forts. From these locations Dutch traders directly interacted with woodland Indians gathering beaver fur for the European hat market.

As the system evolved it became apparent that not all the trading forts were performing with equal profitability. Fort Orange in Albany, New York, with its direct access to Manhattan via the Hudson River, emerged as the dominant location for procuring fur. The Mohawk River, which flowed into the Hudson above Albany, penetrated deep into the interior of Mohawk territory with its abundant beaver habitat.

The consequence of the success of Fort Orange meant fewer resources were available for Fort Good Hope in Hartford, Connecticut, and the forts of the Delaware River at the southern edge of New Netherland. As a result, Fort Good Hope and control of the Connecticut River soon fell to the English. Additionally, the ramshackle Dutch fort, Fort Nassau, near Camden, New Jersey, was left abandoned, creating an opportunity for the Swedes to establish their own colony on the Delaware.

New Sweden's control of the Delaware River threatened the fur trade in New Netherland, since the Delaware provided an alternate route to the Mohawks in the heartland of New York. In 1651, what was left of Fort Nassau was dismantled by the Dutch. In its place, many miles south on the western shore of the Delaware, Fort Casimir was built. It was no marvel of military engineering, but it didn't have to be since its primary function was to re-establish a trading post and strategically secure Dutch authority on the river.

After the fall of New Sweden, and as the beaver trade diminished, Fort Casimir, and the growing community that adjoined it, evolved into an interactive trading partner with dissatisfied English farmers in Virginia and Maryland. Tobacco was the principle cash crop. High taxes and harsh laws provided the incentive for burdened English growers to trade with the neighboring Dutch.

Once the English understood the commercial and strategic value of the Manhattan centered Dutch colony, and began totaling the losses incurred by competitive tobacco trading in New Netherland, it was simply a matter of time before action would be taken. Seizing the Dutch colony would join the Massachusetts colony with the well established and profitable Virginia colony giving England complete control over a vast area of North America. With little in the way of justification King Charles II gave New Netherland to his brother. In 1664 the Duke of York's warships and soldiers claimed his gift.

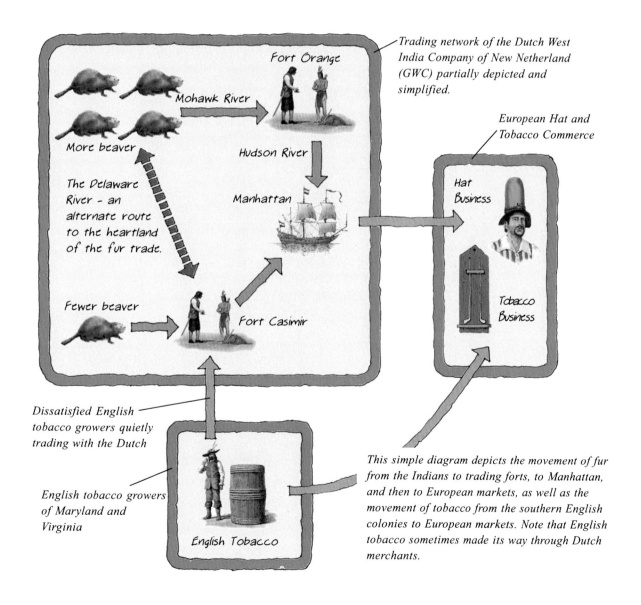

Trading network of the Dutch West India Company of New Netherland (GWC) partially depicted and simplified.

European Hat and Tobacco Commerce

Fort Orange

Mohawk River

More beaver

Hudson River

The Delaware River - an alternate route to the heartland of the fur trade.

Manhattan

Hat Business

Fewer beaver

Fort Casimir

Tobacco Business

Dissatisfied English tobacco growers quietly trading with the Dutch

English tobacco growers of Maryland and Virginia

English Tobacco

This simple diagram depicts the movement of fur from the Indians to trading forts, to Manhattan, and then to European markets, as well as the movement of tobacco from the southern English colonies to European markets. Note that English tobacco sometimes made its way through Dutch merchants.

"The fort is situated in an untenable place where it was located on the first discovery of New Netherland for the purpose of resisting any attack of barbarians rather than an assault of European arms."

Petrus Stuyvesant, 1664

Excerpt from a 1664 letter sent by Petrus Stuyvesant to the Directors of the Dutch West India Company following the capture of New Netherland by the English. The fort Stuyvesant is referring to is Fort Amsterdam in Manhattan, although he could be easily writing about all the forts built in the colony.

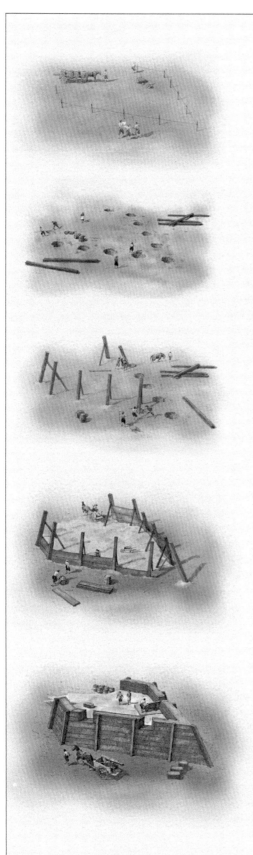

2.

The Bastion

The following section depicts the construction of a hypothetical planked bastion. The exact technique and sequence of assembly may never be known. Basic carpentry, however, remains fundamentally the same as it was in the 17th century and since most early North American forts were made primarily of wood, it is possible to credibly approximate a semblance of what may have been. The speculative example given here is only one possibility.

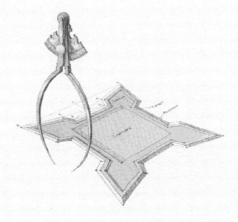

Fortification Design
Star Fort on the Delaware

by Peter A. Douglas

FOUR BASTION FORT

Clearly the most outstanding feature of the forts of New Netherland are the bastions, those pointed parts of the fortifications that project like spear tips from the ramparts. The first time I saw the plan of one of these 17th century Dutch forts, a curious image jumped into my mind. The image was from feudal Japan, of all places, a culture so disconnected from New Netherland by time and distance that it made me smile. What flashed into my head was the picture of a *shuriken*, a ninja throwing star. The similarity is superficial, I grant, but among the many designs of this weapon there is such a star with four pointed blades that resembles the triangular corner bastions of many forts all over the world, including those erected by the Dutch in America. On an early spring afternoon, Len and I spent three hours talking about the construction of such fortifications, and that of Fort Casimir in particular.

In 1986, Edward and Louise Heite conducted an archaeological and historical investigation of Fort Casimir. In their report the Heites wrote: "There is no reason to suppose that the fort differed radically from the Dutch forts at Albany, Manhattan, or Recife, Brazil." By the time that Fort Casimir was built, the architecture of such forts was well established, and Casimir's close neighbor, Fort Christina, was of the same design. In fact, even a century later in the 1750s numerous military installations (such as Fort Stanwix and Fort Ticonderoga in New York) were, with geographic and other necessary deviations, built from the same basic blueprint, though of more enduring materials. Of similar "star" design, though on a much vaster scale, is Fort George, near Inverness, completed in 1769 to pacify the Scottish highlands following the Jacobite rising of 1745.

Len has not been to Brazil, but he has thoroughly researched Fort Orange (Albany) and Fort Amsterdam (Manhattan), and painted both forts many times, so he is very familiar with these structures. He was thus able to approach an investigation of Fort Casimir with a running start, augmenting his knowledge with extensive reading of current books and contemporary accounts, the latter never failing to fascinate.

Searching for confirmation of the Heites' reasonable supposition concerning the fort's configuration, Len examined again the only extant depiction of it, Lindström's questionable sketch. Bearing in mind what is known of Dutch fort design and of the unique situation of this fort, Len applied this to Lindström's view of Casimir. Given the marshy area in which the fort was built, the need for some sort of solid base was called for. Len theorized that what is behind the "riverfront wall" in the Swede's drawing is not part of the fort itself; what is depicted, he believes, is actually the front elevation of the foundation, or "platform," on which the fort itself was erected. This platform covered an area larger than the fort, and probably consisted of a massive accumulation of earth, sod, wood, and rubble, sufficient to contain the unstable ground and raise the surface out of the swamp to create a firm foundation. In itself, this is an impressive civil engineering achievement.

As for the actual fort on top of this, if we look again more carefully at Lindström's flat elevation we can see that he has attempted to provide some depth to the drawing by shading two sections of the curtain wall that lies beneath the interior buildings. Knowing what to look for from an understanding of other contemporary forts, it's easy to agree with Len when he posits that these hatch marks represents the flanks and shoulders of the fort's two bastions that faced the river.

A bastion, then, is the part of a fort's defensive system that projects outward from the ramparts, often located where the curtain walls meet. They provide for active defense against assaulting troops. One bastion enables defenders to cover adjacent bastions and walls with defensive fire. Fort Casimir's other two bastions cannot be seen in Lindström's one-dimensional depiction, but the standard symmetry of contemporary fortifications means that we can confidently infer their existence.

To show this, Len created a computer model of Casimir that can be nimbly tilted and viewed from any angle. One minute we view the fort as an attacker would, approaching at ground level, creeping carefully up the imaginary glacis, and then we soar over the plan of it like birds. This overhead view shows the now familiar square star-shaped construction with sharp pointed bastions in each corner, the walls containing a reconstruction of the living quarters, stores, and other buildings. From such electronic models and sketches Len has produced the likeness

of the fort found in this book. This basic "star" format has been used in numerous countries, and in some instances forts had multiple bastions and developed into extremely elaborate and beautiful almost organic flower-like structures. They can be explored on maps and sometimes on foot even today.

The principle of the bastion comes from the medieval castle. Advances in military technology led to the increasing vulnerability and the decline of these towering fortresses of the Middle Ages whose great height was their main advantage. Vulnerability to powder and shot, and particularly to large maneuverable siege cannon, led to the development of fortified positions with lower walls that were embedded in ditches fronted by earthen slopes that could absorb shot. However, low walls meant that they could be more easily stormed, so military architecture had to change again. Especially unhelpful were the previously dominant rounded turrets; these created "dead zones" that sheltered attackers from the defenders' fire. To counter this, round or square turrets were extended outwards to form diamond-shaped points that eliminated these indefensible areas. To increase the effectiveness of the lower walls, the shape was designed to make maximum use of enfilade, or flanking fire, at any enemy who reached the walls. Bastion-mounted cannon had a clear line of fire directly down the curtain wall to the neighboring bastion, preventing a close assault.

The need to defend a fort with a lower profile was offset by creating, where feasible, larger impregnable areas that provided defense in depth, where attackers had to overcome several layers of defenses. In the case of Fort Casimir, the tidal water and the swamp limited its extent and possibilities for growth, but this natural defensive barrier doubtless made up for the difficulties that must have been encountered in its construction in such a place.

These four-bastioned Dutch forts were pretty much the minimalist design for bastion forts. Simplicity of construction stemmed, certainly in the case of Casimir, from the necessary use of accessible local materials, principally earth and timber. There were no convenient quarries for stone, and no knowledgeable masons at hand, and there seems to have been no interest in establishing such ambitious structures, especially in view of how the Swedes and the Dutch were playing constant leapfrog with their forts in the Delaware estuary to assert their national interests.

In the world of military architecture we must think of Fort Casimir as something basic, even primitive. It was the product of much sweat and labor but while it was hardly a serious defensible redoubt, it nevertheless fulfilled the role of establishing a national presence. It was a frontier outpost, more easily compared with the 19th century "Fort Apaches" of the western plains. Casimir was not intended to be as imposing, elegant, or enduring as some of the North American English forts of the mid-18th century. There are clear design similarities, for the basic principles still largely applied, but so many of these latter forts survive because they were built of stone. Casimir was constructed of wood and dirt, and to remain in an efficient working condition such a structure required perpetual upkeep and repair, neither of which was lavished on Casimir. It had fared poorly by the time the Swedes took it over, only three years after it had been built. In addition to neglect, the rigors of the Mid-Atlantic environment and the fundamental method of construction conspired to reduce the fort to a run-down condition that was never rectified while it was in Dutch hands.

Winter's freezing and thawing heaved and warped the posts and planks of the bastions, while rain rusted the nails and made the earthen fill sodden and heavy. Water and liquefied earth would have been squeezed out between the retaining planks causing serious instability. Insects were constantly at work, while the humid summers encouraged the growth of seeds, and raised weeds and saplings that would have quickly taken root. One can just imagine how, after a couple of seasons, the fort would have taken on an overgrown and ruined appearance that the inadequate and unhappy garrison could hardly have prevented. There could be little resistance to the attack by English warships in 1664, which hastened the fort's total destruction. Before long its shattered remains rotted into the Delaware mud and Casimir became a memory, of interest not to tourists but to historians and archaeologists—and to artists.

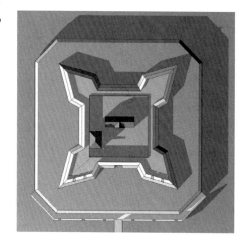

P. A. Douglas, 2011

The Beautiful and the Deadly
Europe's Grand Designs and American Realities

The age old design of the medieval fortress could not provide an acceptable level of defense against the powerful new weapons of the 17th century. Engineers realized that rounded, high-walled turrets had become obsolete. Cylindrical turrets created triangulated areas along the fort wall which provided cover for an attacker. A new geometry was needed based on "fields of fire" from multiple cannon positions. The diagonal diamond-shaped bastion emerged as the obvious solution.

Marshal Sebastien Le Prestre de Vauban was perhaps the most well known military engineer of the 17th century. France, during the reign of Louis XIV, was at war most of the time. Weapons and tactics were changing. "The art of war" required talent and Vauban was there to deliver.

Vauban is credited with taking the already complex process of fort design to its ultimate level of sophistication. His design ideas are noteworthy not only because of the distinct massed structural arrangements of primary fortifications, but also for the elaborate earth works that surrounded them. Conversely, his understanding of defensive geometry made him an effective designer of elaborate siege works as well. The beautiful crystal and flowerlike renditions of these intricate creations belie their deadly purpose for they are extraordinarily pleasing to the eye. Vauban's influence can be seen in military landscape planning for centuries after his death.

With all the accolades Vauban definitely earned, the principles incorporated into his basic philosophical approach to military landscape design were already being applied, albeit somewhat simplified, by Dutch engineers around the globe. Since the Netherlands was a well established international trading nation of great success in the 17th century, the Dutch, out of necessity, had taken the basic concepts of fort building and modified them to meet the very specific needs and conditions they encountered in vastly different environments.

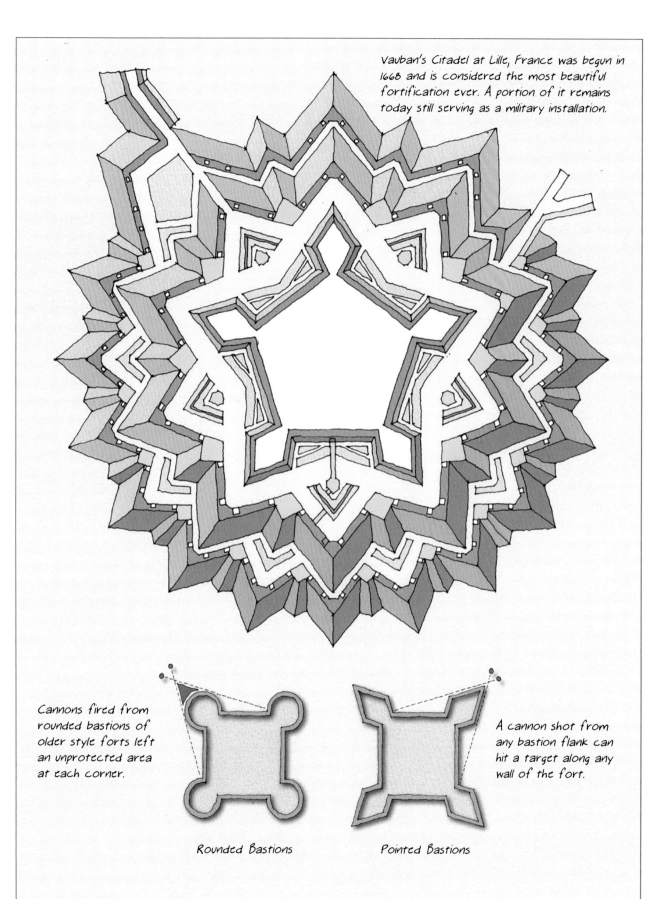

Vauban's Citadel at Lille, France was begun in 1668 and is considered the most beautiful fortification ever. A portion of it remains today still serving as a military installation.

Cannons fired from rounded bastions of older style forts left an unprotected area at each corner.

A cannon shot from any bastion flank can hit a target along any wall of the fort.

Rounded Bastions

Pointed Bastions

Dutch Forts in North America
Building Basic Defenses

The Dutch built massive stone forts in the Netherlands, Asia, the Caribbean, and numerous other locations. The construction of these durable structures reflected the economic and strategic value of those locations and the threat levels they faced from their enemies. These forts were expensive to build and maintain, requiring large work forces from the onset. North America was a very different case. The fur trade was nowhere near the monetary importance of the spice or sugar trade. Labor in New Netherland was limited and amounted to the men that could be supplied by the Dutch West India Company itself. Forts needed to provide basic security at low cost and with a minimal amount of construction time. Wood and dirt were the plentiful materials. The sites for these forts were usually on or near soggy river banks. The engineering of these facilities was basic, but the conceptual design bore the unmistakable mark of experienced technicians.

The forts on the Hudson, Delaware, and Connecticut Rivers were simple. Initially, the idea of building a five-bastion stone fort in Manhattan was considered, but in the end it, too, was built as a four-bastion fort. In some locations, like the Fort of Good Hope, on the Connecticut River, the entire fortification was no more than a house with a wall around it.

In this section we will explore one possible approach to the construction of a corner bastion of a simple wooden fort. The planked design seems to have been common in forts the Dutch built in Albany and in Manhattan. There are a few period drawings and some correspondence that indicate a procedure of this nature could have been employed. This is a speculative scenario which may bring up as many questions as it answers, but it does attempt to deal with issues that have, for too long, been left unaddressed. Since neither Fort Casimir nor Fort Amsterdam in Manhattan were built with surrounding ditches, that feature will not be presented in this hypothetical example.

Fort Orange was originally built in 1624. It was modified several times over its life span of approximately 80 years. English alterations in the 1670's substantially altered the bastion surface appearance, but the overall shape of the fort was retained. Unlike Fort Casimir and Fort Amsterdam, Fort Orange was surrounded by a defensive ditch.

Fort Orange, Rensselaerswijck, circa 1650

Fort Amsterdam was built in 1626. Like Fort Orange it was modified many times. In 1633, Wouter van Twiller ordered that the bastions be rebuilt in stone. In the end only the northwest bastion was upgraded. In 1664, after the English takeover of New Netherland, the fort was renamed Fort George. It was substantially improved and survived for a total of 164 years. The footprint of the original Dutch fort was still visible on New York City maps in 1790.

The Northwest Bastion of Fort Amsterdam

Fort Amsterdam, Manhattan, circa 1655
Note that the northwest bastion (far left) is built of stone unlike the others.

Engineering and Surveying
The Tools of the Trade

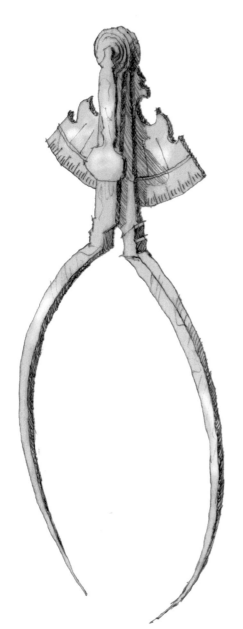

Complex architectural and engineering projects are worked out on paper long before a shovel goes in the ground. Although techniques have improved, human ingenuity has remained constant. The devices employed to solve geometrical problems in the 17th century were effective and accurate. An impressive collection of drafting instruments at the Museo Galileo in Milan, Italy, dating from the mid 1600's contains compasses and protractors, easily identified and familiar to us today. There are, however, many other specialized and totally alien measurement tools in the collection, the uses of which elude us today. Similarly, field surveying had its own set of issues requiring clever solutions. The ancestor of the modern digital surveyor's transit was a surveyor's compass. Some beautifully crafted brass instruments of that time survive in museum collections. The more common wooden designs are rarer but do appear in 17th century drawings. The study of these reveals dozens of tools employed by military engineers in laying out fortifications. A few noteworthy examples are depicted here.

A 17th century protractor and compass from a collection in Florence, Italy. These precision instruments have changed very little over the last three hundred years.

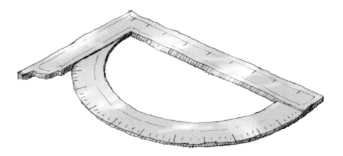

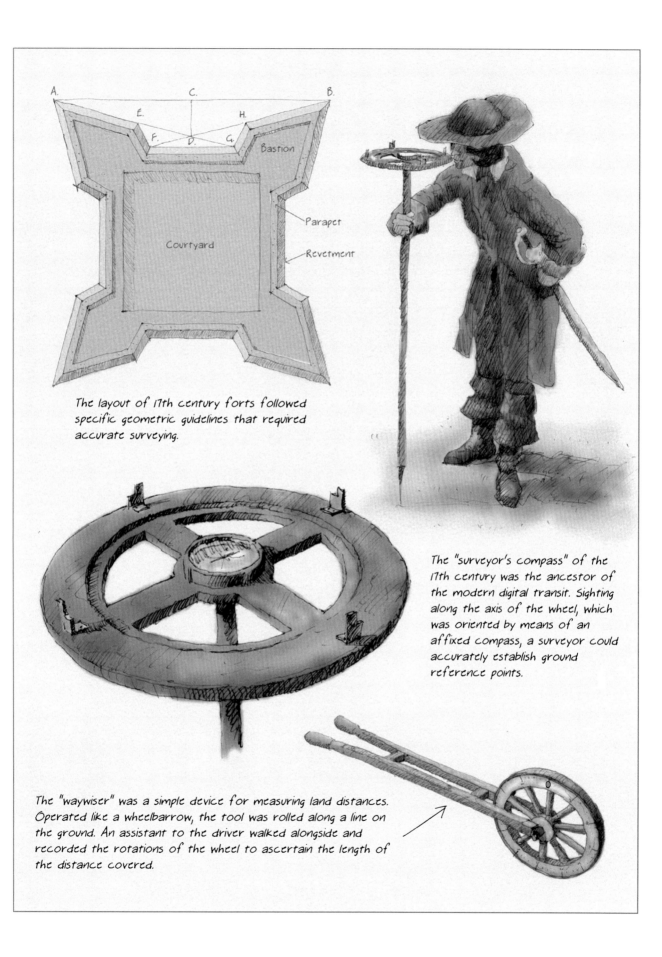

A. C. B.
E. H.
F. D. G.
Bastion
Parapet
Courtyard
Revetment

The layout of 17th century forts followed specific geometric guidelines that required accurate surveying.

The "surveyor's compass" of the 17th century was the ancestor of the modern digital transit. Sighting along the axis of the wheel, which was oriented by means of an affixed compass, a surveyor could accurately establish ground reference points.

The "waywiser" was a simple device for measuring land distances. Operated like a wheelbarrow, the tool was rolled along a line on the ground. An assistant to the driver walked alongside and recorded the rotations of the wheel to ascertain the length of the distance covered.

Bastion Construction
Stage 1. Site Preparation

Once the plans for the fort were finalized construction could begin. The first step was to advantageously locate the fort on the site, assuming that this had not already been established during the planning stage. Numerous critical factors were considered. Strategic sight lines, terrain elevation, proximity to potable water, and access to supply routes would have been at the top of the hierarchical list. The later element, access to supply routes, for the Dutch meant a location that could be serviced from a navigable waterway with sufficient depth to accommodate large cargo and military vessels.

Site preparation began with the removal of large rocks, trees, stumps, and brush. If necessary, the terrain was cut or filled to achieve a somewhat level plain on which to build. Surveyors would then locate the key perimeter points of the fort. Each point would be marked by driving wooden stakes into the ground. Ropes were then tied to the stakes clearly defining the outline of the fort on the ground. In addition to marking points of intersection, the stakes also demarked the center points of foundation excavations for major structural elements. The land was now ready for excavation.

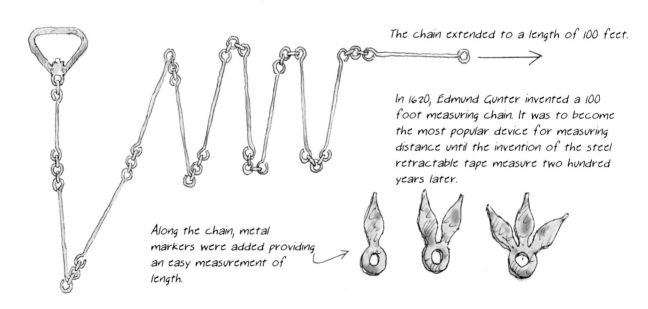

The chain extended to a length of 100 feet.

In 1620, Edmund Gunter invented a 100 foot measuring chain. It was to become the most popular device for measuring distance until the invention of the steel retractable tape measure two hundred years later.

Along the chain, metal markers were added providing an easy measurement of length.

BASTION CONSTRUCTION
STAGE 1 - LAYING OUT THE PERIMETER

Using what were the sophisticated surveying instruments of the time, key perimeter points of a bastion could be established and marked with stakes and ropes.

Fort Casimir was probably designed as a simple four-bastion fort like this.

This is an idealized version of a basic four-bastioned fort using the conventional geometrical design rules of the 17th century. By 1670, Vauban was emerging as the pre-eminent engineer in the field of military fortification planning. Many of the principles that he would later refine were already in use by the Dutch.

Approximating the size of Fort Casimir, and incorporating established geometrical rules, the dimensions of all facets of the fort's layout can be determined, including the general scale of the structures within the fort.

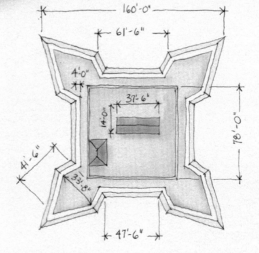

Bastion Construction

Stage 2. Excavation

Once the post hole locations had been established, workers set about the arduous task of excavation. Using simple tools they broke ground, chopped through roots, and removed stones and other impediments as required for each bastion. Holes needed to be dug to a depth of approximately one quarter the length of the upright post in order to provide sufficient support. Softer or sandier soils meant deeper holes. Under average conditions a twenty foot bastion post would necessitate a foundation hole of approximately five feet in depth. Although the foundations of planked wooden forts took some time to prepare, it was a minimal effort when compared to the labor needed in the construction of stone forts of that period. It took fewer men and vastly less time to build with wood and soil. The great disadvantages were in the substantial maintenance required and the vulnerability of unfinished wood to decay.

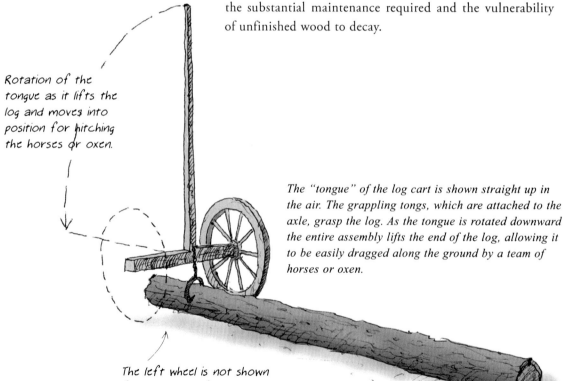

Rotation of the tongue as it lifts the log and moves into position for hitching the horses or oxen.

The "tongue" of the log cart is shown straight up in the air. The grappling tongs, which are attached to the axle, grasp the log. As the tongue is rotated downward the entire assembly lifts the end of the log, allowing it to be easily dragged along the ground by a team of horses or oxen.

The left wheel is not shown for the sake of clarity.

Bastion Construction
Stage 2 - Excavation And Site Preparation

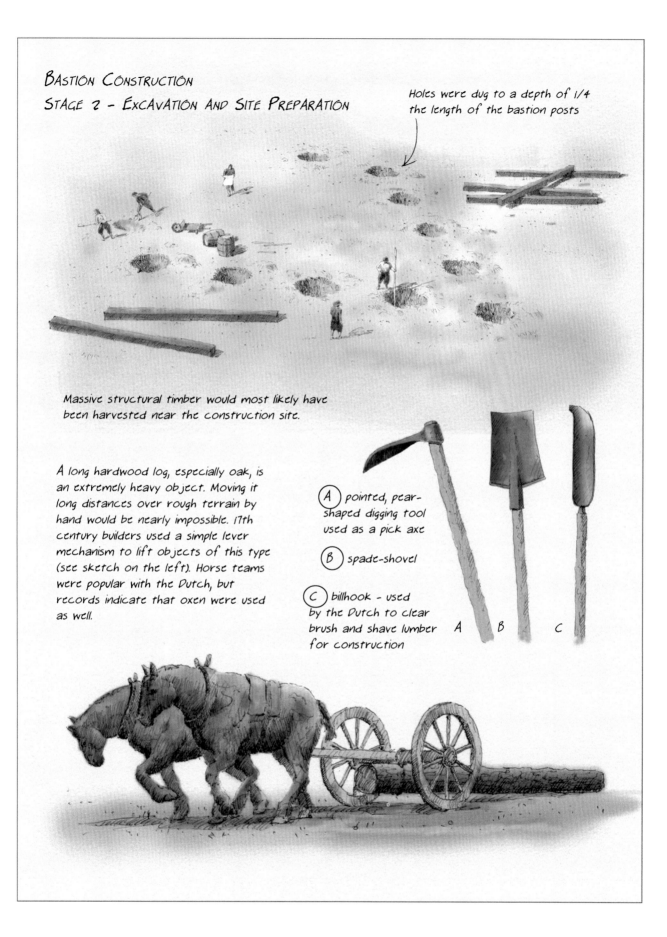

Holes were dug to a depth of 1/4 the length of the bastion posts

Massive structural timber would most likely have been harvested near the construction site.

A long hardwood log, especially oak, is an extremely heavy object. Moving it long distances over rough terrain by hand would be nearly impossible. 17th century builders used a simple lever mechanism to lift objects of this type (see sketch on the left). Horse teams were popular with the Dutch, but records indicate that oxen were used as well.

A) pointed, pear-shaped digging tool used as a pick axe

B) spade-shovel

C) billhook - used by the Dutch to clear brush and shave lumber for construction

A   B   C

Bastion Construction
Stage 3. The Posts

Delaware had an abundance of mature trees in the 17th century suitable for structural lumber. An experienced carpenter from Europe would already know the advantages and disadvantages of some of the native species. The common varieties for construction would have been loblolly pine (southern yellow pine), red oak, and white oak. Ash and hickory were in good supply and possessed many of the characteristics of sturdy hardwoods, but they did not have the durability of oak and yellow pine. Given the frequency of period comments regarding the decay of fort walls, it's possible that these woods may have been tried and failed to meet expectations for resisting the ravages of moisture and insects. In actuality, oak and pine fared only slightly better.

Oak and yellow pine were enormous straight grained trees reaching heights, at that time, of 80 to 100 feet. Felling lumber of this size was a task for only the most skilled woodsmen. Native people are said to have "girdled" large pine trees, that is to cut away the life sustaining bark around the trunk, thereby killing the tree. They then allowed the timber to "dry on the stump." After a sufficient time passed the tree was taken down. With the wood partially seasoned the logs were lighter and easier to move. There is no record of Europeans using this technique. Their approach was most likely to strategically drop large trees using axes and then divide them into manageable lengths to be dragged away by horses or oxen.

Lumber was squared off with hand tools like the axe and the adze. Unlike sawn timber, hand squared logs were shaped by eye and varied with the skill of the woodsmen. For the sake of our hypothetical bastion, the length of the average finished post will be 20 feet. This would allow a post buried in the ground 5 feet to project 15 feet above the surface. The exact finished lengths would vary slightly with placement, due to the varying angles needed to achieve the sloping walls of the finished structure. In order to hold the post in place while the hole was being backfilled with dirt, bracing timber called "shoring" may have been used.

Bastion walls were sloped inward as they rise above the ground to reduce the pressure of the earth fill at the top of the structure. A straight wall has a tendency to tip outward from the force of soil especially when it is wet.

Posts were tipped into holes and then hoisted into position by horses and men.

A common and indispensable tool on construction sites for over 2,000 years was the wheelbarrow, which originated in China. This 17th century wooden version varies little from a modern wheelbarrow.

The Colonial Wheelbarrow

Squaring a log with an axe was achieved by first chopping vertical kerfs along a line followed by parallel strokes down the side, creating a flat surface. The process may or may not have been repeated on all four faces depending on the usage and preference of the builder.

Planks from Fort Orange
Milling Lumber in Rensselaerswijck

Records contained in "New York Historical Manuscripts: Dutch, volumes XVIII through XIX, Delaware Papers," translated by Charles T. Gehring, indicate requests for, and delivery of, thousands of board feet of planks to New Amstel (New Castle, DE) from Fort Orange (Albany, NY) in the 1650's. The flat terrain of Delaware made water powered sawmills infeasible, unlike the hilly landscape of the Hudson Valley. Using milled lumber dramatically reduced construction time, since the alternative was hand sawing with a two-man pit saw. In 1637, Pieter Cornelisen and Albert Andriesen Bradt built the first successful sawmill in the colony of Rensselaerswijck (Albany, NY). Bradt assumed complete control of the mill in 1646, and operated it until 1672. The Bradt mill was probably the source for milled lumber in colonial Delaware. In addition to planks, records indicate the shipment of tons of Fort Orange bricks to New Castle. It seems likely that ships loaded with wood were probably ballasted with bricks.

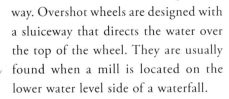

This schematic drawing on the left illustrates the general operating mechanism of a 17th century sawmill. Although many details have been omitted, the primary working parts are shown. Water passes on the underside of the wheel causing it to rotate. That rotation is then converted by means of several wooden gears to a crankshaft, which in turn moves a set of saw blades, set into a frame, up and down, thereby cutting several planks from a log at the same time. The log is secured to a moving carriage which advances it through the saw. When water passes underneath the wheel it is referred to as an "undershot" wheel. The Bradt sawmill was set up in this way. Overshot wheels are designed with a sluiceway that directs the water over the top of the wheel. They are usually found when a mill is located on the lower water level side of a waterfall.

The Bradt sawmill was located on the Normanskill in Albany, NY. Its appearance is unknown. This image represents one possibility. It's based on a 17th century Dutch painting of a mill with an undershot wheel.

Albert Bradt's Sawmill on the Normanskill
Rensselaerswijck, circa 1660

Sawn planks were stacked in sheds or barns and allowed to dry slowly. For local use, boards would simply have been carted off in wagons. Fort Orange lumber was also sent off to distant sites in New Netherland and beyond. This lumber would have been stacked in the holds of ships such as the yacht to the left. The diagram below gives an example of a 50 foot Dutch galliot loaded with planks and bricks.

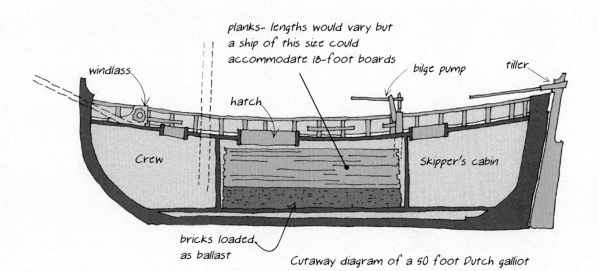

planks- lengths would vary but a ship of this size could accommodate 18-foot boards

windlass

bilge pump

tiller

hatch

Crew

Skipper's cabin

bricks loaded as ballast

Cutaway diagram of a 50 foot Dutch galliot

Bastion Construction
Stage 4. Planking and Filling

After all the posts were set, milled planks were cut and nailed on the back face of the uprights. This method is clearly visible in the depiction of several forts in the Caribbean during this time period. The obvious advantage to proceeding in this manner was that as the bastion was filled, the pressure of the soil would provide additional support for the planks.

Using our hypothetical bastion design as an example, the volume of earth required to fill and finish it would be 14,000 cubic feet of dirt. That is the equivalent of 350 cart loads of soil, or 3,500 wheelbarrow loads. Soil can weigh from 75 to 120 pounds per cubic foot depending on composition and moisture. Considering the marshy land along the Delaware River, this volume of earth could weigh 1,680,000 pounds, or 840 tons. Keep in mind that Fort Casimir, as well as nearly all the other forts of that time had four bastions. That's four times the soil in our calculations. The man hours needed to accomplish this work were substantial. The fill material would have most likely come from an area of the site pre-designated as a defensive trench or a building foundation. Fill may have even been cut from the immediate fort area itself if significant grading were required to level the land. Although this seems like a massive effort it would have been little more than part of normal fortification work. Earthmoving at fort sites took place in all countries on every continent in every century.

It is also interesting to note that hand forged square nails were in common use on construction sites in the 17th century. Records indicate the delivery of thousands of nails to New Netherland. Iron nails are commonly found by archeologists in Dutch excavations. There were hundreds of other ways for carpenters at that time to join wood. Variations of mortise and tenon and the use of wooden pegs would have made up most of them, and were definitely among the array of techniques used in erecting forts.

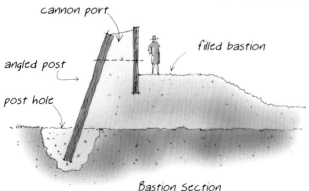

Bastion Section

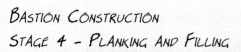

Milled planks were most likely nailed to the back faces of the upright posts.

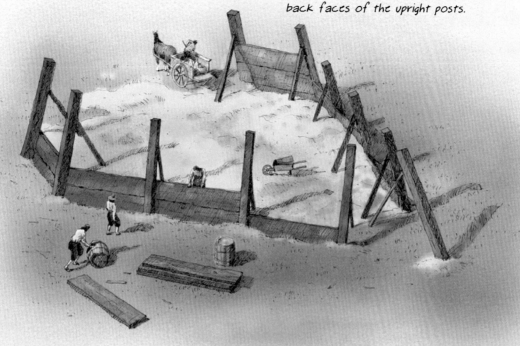

The two-man saw on trestle sawhorses could be used to make planks from logs. Although slow and tedious, this method would have to suffice if work was to continue while awaiting a delivery of milled lumber.

The Dutch, along with all colonial Europeans, kept African slaves. Accounts of the Delaware settlements indicate that they made up a small part of the population, working on farms and plantations and also as non-military personnel in Fort Casimir.

Trestles were repositioned as sawing progressed.

Sawing planks in this manner was hard work. The sawyer, on top, directed the blade. The pitman, on the bottom, did the hard part.

Bastion Construction
Stage 5. Completed Planking

It's possible that the Dutch forts, Fort Casimir included, may have been considered complete when the planked walls were high enough to protect a soldier standing on the earth fill of the bastion. Although the wall would stop an arrow it would provide little defense against cannons and muskets. At the time, hostile natives were considered to be the only threat. As the years passed more formidable foes presented themselves. In 1654, when the Swedes took Fort Casimir from the Dutch, Governor Johan Risingh's journal and the records of military engineer Per Lindeström mention the fort's poor condition and its design shortcomings. They go on to describe alterations they are making to generally improve the bastions and outer defenses. Although the parapets (top of bastion walls) are not specifically mentioned they are clearly depicted in Lindeström's drawing as massively wide structures with cannon ports (embrasures) cut in at intervals.

Access to the bastions from the courtyard of the forts would have been via earthen ramps. Stairs may also have been included. Not all bastions were filled solid with earth. Some bastions were fitted with inner rooms built underneath. These spaces served special needs, most likely as powder magazines.

It is not known exactly what specie or species of wood was used to construct these forts. The assumption is that oak was the preferred material. However, availability and experimentation may have led to the use of other hardwoods and conifers. Whatever the variety, no finishes were applied to the completed structures. The ravages of weather and insects quickly began the process of decay. Cracks and spaces between boards allowed vegetation to take root. Maintaining these walls would have been required continuously. This is borne out by the frequency of requests in fort records for the funding of repairs. Even a short lapse in upkeep would rapidly lead to catastrophic damage and completely undermine the effectiveness of the fort.

Carpenter ants, termites, and other wood devouring insects caused more devastation to the wooden forts of North America than any military siege.

There are dozens of variations in the construction of 17th-century fort bastions. This one, with a partial stone base, is finished with a formed sod top and parapet, backed by a stone retaining wall. The Dutch forts of New Netherland were almost always made of wood with earthen fill.

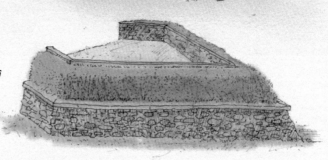

Rooms were sometimes built under bastions.

Not all bastions were completely filled with earth. Brick or stone-lined rooms were sometimes built underneath and used as storage areas. A space of this type was most often used as a powder magazine.

Bastion Construction
Stage 6. Completed Bastion

The final features to complete the bastion would be the construction of the parapet and the fitting of embrasures. Embrasures were flared ports cut into the parapet to facilitate a protected opening from which to fire a cannon. Fort Casimir apparently included many of them. Lindeström's drawing shows embrasures not only along the bastion parapet, but also on top of a defensive outer wall that possibly surrounded the fort. Parapets in the more substantial stone forts of Europe and Asia were massive. The hypothetical bastion represented here is based on the scale of Fort Casimir. The depth of this parapet is 4 feet. The overall bastion itself is too small to accommodate anything much wider. The military standard of the day, in the ideally designed fort, was a parapet 18 feet thick. According to Christopher Duffy, in his book "Fire and Stone," this quantity of earth was sufficient to stand up to the most powerful weapons of that time. A shot from a 24 pound siege cannon would penetrate 15 feet of light soil and 12 feet of more resistant soil. A musket ball's greatest penetration was about 30 inches. It's clear from this data that the Dutch forts of North America would have stood little chance against a full scale military attack from a well-equipped enemy.

Fort Casimir, along with all the other northeastern American forts of the early to mid 17th century, were lightly armed. The cannons they possessed were often an odd mix of weapons from a variety of sources. The Jesuit priest, Father Isaac Jogues, when describing the armaments at Fort Orange in Rensselaerswijck in 1643, states that the "wretched little fort" contains four or five pieces of Breteuil cannons and as many swivel guns. Cannon caliber is not mentioned, although it is assumed that these were small guns. A "three pounder" cannon, said to have been from Fort Orange, is on display at the New York State Museum in Albany. In June of 1654, in describing the improvements made to Fort Casimir (Trinity), Governor Risingh mentions the acquisition of two pairs of "twelve pounder" cannons from the ship "Eagle." These weapons and the small complement of soldiers assigned to that fort would have been capable of only meager resistance against any well armed attack.

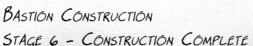

BASTION CONSTRUCTION
STAGE 6 - CONSTRUCTION COMPLETE

Parapets with sod fill and embrasures for cannon

Please note that for the purpose of this hypothetical study, the curtain walls that would join four bastions like this have been omitted. Bastions such as this would not stand alone.

Although many of the Dutch forts were lightly armed, Fort Casimir, during the brief period of Swedish occupation, was initially supplied with four 12 pounders from the ship "Eagle."

Embrasure

Stone base supports wooden deck planks.

Platforms were needed to support the weight of heavy cannons.

"Whereas the honorable lord Jacquet has examined the condition of the fort, Casemier.... inspected the same and found the fort to be completely decayed in its walls and batteries."

Minutes of Jean Paul Jacquet

Christmas Day, 1655

Excerpts from the Minutes of the Administration of Jean Paul Jacquet, Vice-Director of the South River, reporting on the conditions of Fort Casimir following its capture from Sweden. He notes in detail the faults of the failing fort, however there is little evidence that any substantive renovations were ever carried out.

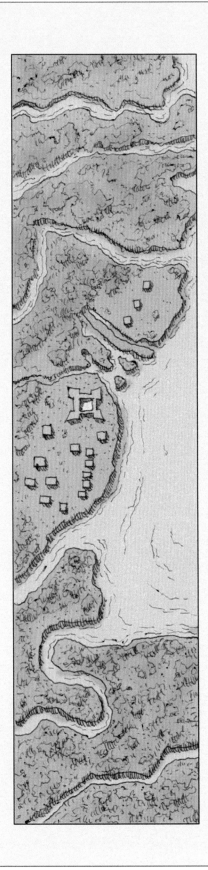

3.

Fort Casimir

Fort Casimir was built by the Dutch in 1651, under the direction of Petrus Stuyvesant. In 1654, it was captured by the Swedes and re-named Fort Trinity. After only four hundred and sixty-six days the fort was re-taken by the Dutch and reverted back to its original name of Fort Casimir. The swamp that adjoined the fort and settlement of Sandhook, later named New Amstel and finally New Castle, was a breeding ground for disease. This added to the boredom and misery of living on the edge of the frontier with little support from the homeland. In this section we will examine the fort, its alterations and ultimate fate.

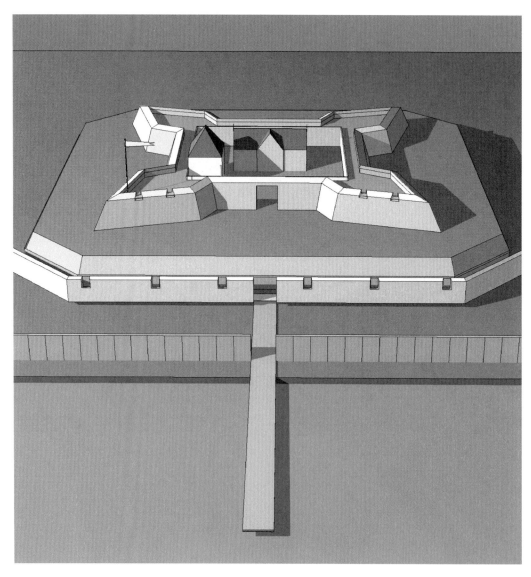

Len Tantillo's digital scale model of Fort Casimir based on Lindeström's elevation drawing, various historical site plans, and the terrain analysis of several topographical studies. Features have been simplified for clarity.

When I began this project I knew very little about Fort Casimir and the colonial history of Delaware. I thought that readers would be interested to know what my earliest preconceptions were in order to appreciate the evolution of the ideas that later emerged. To achieve this I asked my friend Peter Douglas to record our first meeting on Fort Casimir. Since Peter knew as little as I did about the fort he was perfect for the job. What follows is an account of the first step taken in unraveling an interesting historical mystery. - Len Tantillo

The Process of Discovery
A Commentary on the Visualization of Fort Casimir

by Peter A. Douglas

I suppose when Len conceived this project, he and I were at about the same level of unawareness concerning Fort Casimir, though by the time we first spoke of it his research had allowed him to pull ahead by a substantial margin. Nevertheless, for all his prior investigation he said that this would be a "process of discovery" for both of us, and he would like me to be part of this process, observing how he went about it, how research becomes theory, and how theory is transformed into artistic and architectural visualization.

Len already knew, and I was soon to learn, that Fort Casimir had been one of a group of forts constructed on the banks of the Delaware River by the Dutch and the Swedes, who, in the early 17th century, planted their respective flags in the New World. I knew something about the Dutch presence in America, though most of my knowledge, like that of many of us at this end of the colony, I suppose, was of the northern history of New Netherland, around Fort Orange and New Amsterdam. Simple geography had fogged my view somewhat, and this parochial limitation could do with expanding. I knew full well that New Netherland covered a vast area, all the way from present day Delaware to New York and western Connecticut, and I needed to bring the south to the foreground.

Where Fort Casimir was built in 1651 was known to the Dutch settlers as the "Zuyd Rivier," or South River, the southernmost part of New Netherland. Originally it was to be the center of the Dutch North American province, with the capital at High Island in the Delaware, but Director Minuit decided that the North (Hudson)

River would be a better base, and so New Amsterdam became the natural focus. After 1626 the Dutch had built Fort Nassau on the eastern bank of the South River at the site of present-day Gloucester, New Jersey, as a trading and military base. During the brief tussle with the Swedes along the Delaware, a number of forts were constructed, the first Swedish post being Fort Christina, built in 1638, and downriver from the Dutch. And then in 1643, the Swedes under Johan Printz, built their Fort Nya Elfsborg even farther downriver. Thus Dutch ships coming upriver from the bay had to pass these Swedish forts.

When Petrus Stuyvesant, the seventh and last Director of New Netherland, took office in 1647 he wanted to re-assert Dutch control of this region and its lucrative trade. In retaliation for the Swedish encroachment, and recognizing the need for a more propitious site for a fort, Stuyvesant abandoned Fort Nassau in 1651 and, countering the Swedish move in this vast chess game, erected Fort Casimir, named for Ernst Casimir I, Count of Nassau-Dietz and Stadtholder of Friesland, Groningen, and Drenthe, 1573-1632. Being only a few miles south of Fort Christina, it enabled the Dutch to menace the Swedes and interrupt their trade.

Fort Casimir had a short life, and an even shorter one under this name. Relations with the Swedes deteriorated from friction to open hostility, and in 1654 Johan Risingh, the new and last governor of New Sweden, easily captured the fort for the Dutch had not maintained it as a serious strongpoint. Subsequent Swedish reports state that the fort "had fallen into almost total decay," and Risingh wrote that the cannon he found there were "mostly useless." Risingh re-named it *Fort Trefaldighet* (Fort Trinity), and it allowed the Swedes to reassume control of the Delaware. Fort Trinity had a short career too, for in 1655 Stuyvesant returned to New Sweden with a force of several ships and 350 soldiers and retook it. Clearly these forts presented no serious obstacle to capture. Stuyvesant ultimately took Fort Christina, bringing to an end the Swedish presence in America. In 1657 the retaken Fort Casimir (now New Castle) was re-christened New Amstel. Such is the brief career of the subject of this study, which, for much of the time was known as something other than Fort Casimir.

Len first spoke to me of Fort Casimir just after midnight on New Year's Day 2011, after a delightful surfeit of chat, movies, and homemade Chinese food. It was probably not the most propitious time to broach the matter of his project, and wine and exhaustion made me confused and a bit skeptical. Still, I was intrigued, so when Len later proposed an afternoon meeting I was keen to discover more. As anyone who knows Len will tell you, his enthusiasm can be infectious, and so it was for me.

It was some comfort to know that Len regarded my lack of knowledge of the forts of the Delaware (which I readily admitted to) as no impediment to our alliance; it was, he said curiously, a bonus. *Tabula rasa*, I suppose, the strange presumed positive aspect of ignorance, a theory that I've never fully understood. With the zero-degree wind at the windows we sat in his comfortable studio surrounded by books, framed sketches and paintings, ship models, and the cozy aggregation of his diverse artistic treasures. Certainly not the least impressive object in the room was the computer beneath Len's desk, its huge tower the size of a chest of drawers, making a curious technical counterpoint to all the artwork. From its electronic depths a few deft mouse-clicks brought to one of the monitors the only known contemporary image of Fort Casimir, though by then it had become the Swedish Fort Trinity.

Very early in our collaboration, or actually before we could call it that, Len had shown me this drawing of Fort Trinity. The artist was a Swedish engineer called Per Lindström, called in to oversee repairs, and his view of the fort dates from 1655, not long after the Swedes had seized it from the Dutch. At the time of its capture, Fort Casimir was in an appalling state of decay, with a tiny garrison, few cannon, and no powder; it could offer no effective resistance so its taking was a pushover for the Swedes.

Unknown to me at the time, Lindström's drawing is quite an exaggeration, even a work of the imagination. This, even taking into account any repairs and changes that the Swedes undertook. At best it's a stylized version of reality, or an image of the engineer's deepest desire in military architecture, and was doubtless created to impress. Lindström's fort is something like a child's dream of a fort, a solid and impenetrable edifice with what seems to be crenellated stonework bastions housing steep-roofed buildings topped with a fluttering guidon. Stone crenellations also surmount the riverfront wall in front of which stands a sort of wooden palisade and a pier extending into the river.

This is, Len later suggested, a fantasy fort transported from Europe to the American wilderness, and not an accurate depiction of the type of structure of the place or the period. When Len first had me look at Lindström's drawing, it was with no comment, for he wanted to get my own fresh thoughts on it. He was conducting a sort of exercise, an experiment. He said: "Without using any reference, describe what you see in about one or two paragraphs. That drawing is the only image of Fort Casimir ever made during its existence. How does it strike you?" Well I fell for it. I took the drawing at face value, faithfully describing and fleshing out each detail of Lindström's stout and impressive fort in misguided words, not even grasping at the time what should have been so obvious, that the stone battlements, the so imposing and ambitious circumvallation that Lindström depicted, deviated so markedly from the simple Dutch forts of the period that I was familiar with.

Having read my accurate but misconstrued description of the fort, Len responded: "Congratulations. You now have the same preconceived notion of Fort Casimir / Fort Trinity that everybody else has when they begin their study by looking at the only visual evidence of the fort's design. This is our starting point. From here we will look deeper into the mystery of the actual appearance of New Castle, Delaware's first buildings." Error and darkness are the origin of discovery.

Len assured me that the real forts in New Netherland and New Sweden were much less impressive and ambitious. They were very crude, he said, built fast and economically, and consisted largely of raised earthen breastworks and berms reinforced with timber, made, in other words, from the materials at hand. Len has found contemporary documentation that refers to the repair of these forts, and all that was required for that was dirt and wood, available in abundance. The resources of the region did not include quarries for stone for the construction of forts such as Lindström depicted. Len likened this fort to Fort Orange, and Fort Amsterdam in Manhattan, both of which he has studied and painted many times. He quoted a letter from Peter Stuyvesant where he complained that Fort Amsterdam was crumbling away and was even being laid waste by livestock. Clearly these forts were prey to the harsh elements and quickly deteriorated if not diligently maintained. They did not so much represent military power as statements of possession, somewhere to fly the flag and flaunt a bit of in-your-face national pride, and the rate of construction along the Delaware in the middle of the 17th century shows how quickly they could be erected. They were sometimes successful as redoubts in the event of an Indian attack, but they presented no serious obstacle to the overwhelming firepower of armies and navies of the time.

The disturbing fact was, then, that there was only one picture of Fort Casimir and that wasn't much like it really was! This, of course, was the challenge.

Naturally I asked Len, "Why Fort Casimir?" From what little I knew of the forts of the South River, there was at least one other that I'd actually heard of, Fort Christina, so I naturally wondered what was special about Fort Casimir. Len said that Casimir was typical. Not much is known of it, so here was an opportunity to find out more about it. While archaeologists and historians have devoted some attention to it, no credible picture of the fort exists, least of all Lindström's unreliable drawing, along with later derivative, warmed-over depictions that are far too reliant on the Swede's exaggerated elements that were seized upon slavishly and literally.

So, in part, the mystery is the lure. Len told me that he welcomes the opportunity to research and create a more faithful representation of Fort Casimir, to show how these forts were designed and constructed, to bring out a sense of what life was like on the South River then, and to illustrate the inevitable struggle that it was, under the unremitting ravages of the environment and the enemy's harrying, to inhabit and maintain a military installation in that place.

First it was necessary to do two things: work out the design of the fort, and figure out its location. The Heites determined that the site of the fort lay on a sandy hook of land that encroached into a marshy area to the northeast of what would become New Castle, Delaware. Here there was a small sandy hill called Bull Hill, and Fort Casimir was built on the river (east) side of this, then virtually an island in the marsh, at an elevation of about eight feet. The tidal stream and the marsh formed a natural moat on three sides of the fort, which had land access via a ridge that ran southwest. Here, then, was the approximate location of Fort Casimir.

As for what it looked like, Per Lindström wrote that Fort Casimir had been constructed "with four bastions," two of which can be seen in his extravagant front elevation sketch. Despite his overdrawn and idealistic view, there's no reason to disbelieve his statement about the four bastions, which was the usual design for such military earthworks of the time. Len, using his knowledge of other Dutch forts, computer-designed a to-scale four-bastion fort of the appropriate dimensions (the Swedish engineer had thoughtfully provided measurements). Matching the scale image of the star-shaped fort with the contoured survey of the sandy hook of land provided by the Heites, Len was able to place it in position on the hook; it fit perfectly.

That is Peter's account of how the project started. What follows represents months of work and what I came to believe was the actual story of Lindestroms drawing, Fort Casimir, and New Amstel. History will be the judge of its accuracy - Len Tantillo

The Mysterious Drawing of Per Lindeström

In 1655, Per Lindeström created a mysterious drawing. His talent for engineering was a great asset for the repair and re-fortification of the captured Dutch fort at what is now New Castle, Delaware. New Sweden had control of the South River (Delaware River) and all efforts were made to secure its principle settlements. Fort Christina, which is now Wilmington, Delaware, had been carefully sited to defend the small community that lay slightly inland of the fort. Lindeström's drawings of Fort Christina are clear, definitive, and simple. Fort Casimir, renamed Fort Trinity by the Swedes, was a different matter.

The drawing Lindeström made of Fort Casimir's front elevation has lead to many misconceptions as to its actual appearance. In 1905, Alexander B. Cooper, Esq., wrote a paper for the Delaware Historical Society entitled "Fort Casimir, the Starting Point

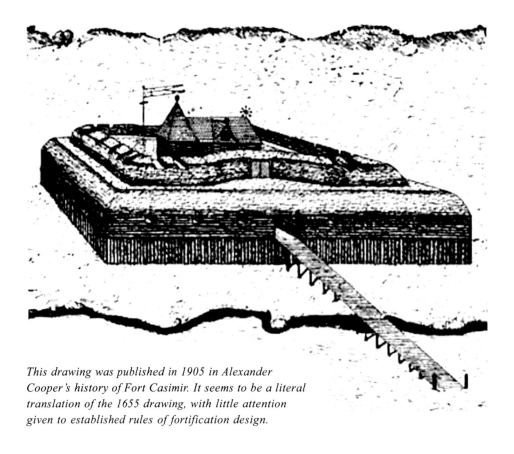

This drawing was published in 1905 in Alexander Cooper's history of Fort Casimir. It seems to be a literal translation of the 1655 drawing, with little attention given to established rules of fortification design.

Note how the gaps at the edges of the fort give the structure the appearance of floating above the elements below it.

gap in the line

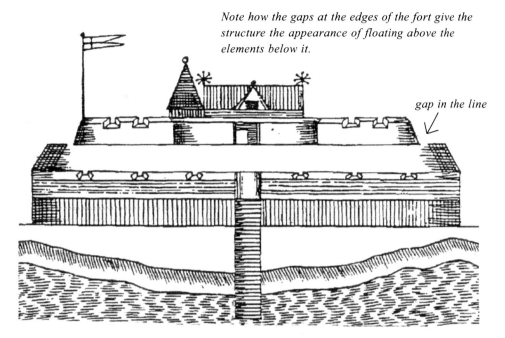

This is a detail from the most commonly referred to reproduction of Per Lindeström's 1655 drawing of Fort Trinity (Casimir).

in the History of New Castle, in the State of Delaware, its Location and History, 1651-1671." Mr. Cooper's book contained a rather awkward pen and ink aerial view that attempted to interpret the original Swedish rendition. In my opinion the artist made some serious errors in judgment. He literally translated the original elevation made by Lindeström into a peculiar, solid, almost square block form without attempting to suggest conventional principles of fort design in general usage in North America at that time. He also ignored other evidence regarding Fort Casimir's appearance clearly visible in the numerous maps that Lindeström made of New Sweden. Many of those drawings show, a plan view of a conventional four-bastion fort at Sandhook.

More recently some researchers have become confused by what appears to be a floating fort above an earthwork, leading them to believe that Fort Casimir/Trinity are two separate forts. This misconception arises from the separation between the upper fort and the lower part of Lindeström's drawing, in the most commonly referenced reproductions of that work. Their conclusion is based on two short ink lines that are missing, a flaw in the reproduction of the drawing that occurred after the original was published.

To make the case that Lindeström's drawing depicts one site with a Dutch four-bastion fort and Swedish improvements to the earth works surrounding it, I submit that in a 1655 sketch for a New Sweden map made by Lindeström, his indication of the fort site is expressed by the four-bastion fort alone, as if the earthworks around it were inconsequential. Also, a book by Thomas Companius Holm, entitled "Kort beskrifning om provincien Nya Swerige uti America: som nu fortjden af the Engelske kallas," Pensylvania Stockholm: J. H. Werner, published in 1702, clearly indicates one single fortification. In other words, there is no gap in the line under the Dutch fort. One last point is that when the poorly reproduced versions of Lindeström's complete drawing are studied, there are numerous gaps in other areas such as lettering and borders, and the omission of many small details. This leads me to believe that the broken lines were not intentional.

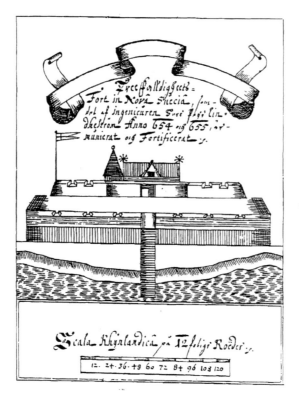

Elevations of this type were often created to serve as navigational aids.

The reproduction of Lindeström's drawing most often referred to appears on the left. The reproduction on the right is taken from Holm's book on the history of New Sweden, published in 1702. The drawing on the left was most likely traced from the 1702 book plate. Note that the title banner at the top of the plate has been omitted in the later version. Also noteworthy is the number of broken lines, the additional text, and the repositioning of the scale bar in the traced piece.

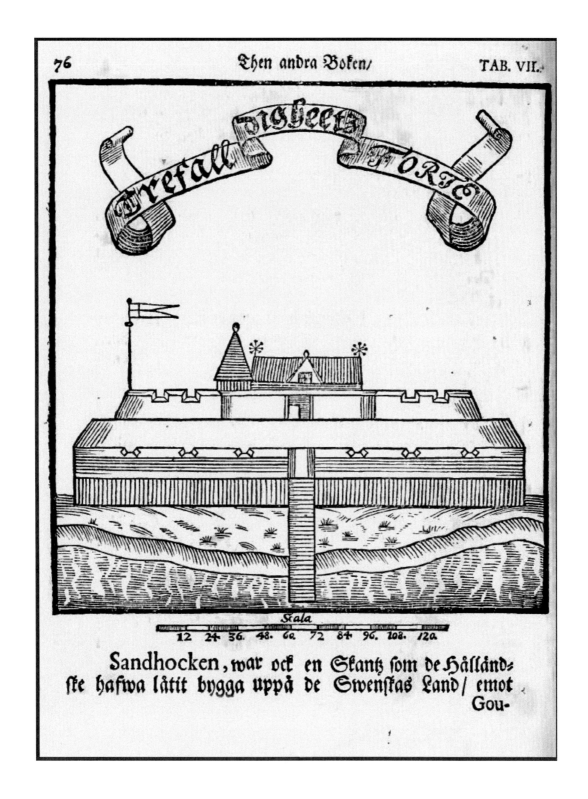

An Interpretation of the Lindeström Drawing

The interpretation of the Lindeström elevation drawing of Fort Casimir, which the Swedes had renamed Fort Trinity, is the key to truly understanding its design configuration. Several artists and historians have attempted to explain the two-dimensional head-on view made in 1655, with little or no agreement as to its salient features. So here is, yet again, another possibility.

I began my theory with a careful consideration of the established fortification design principles of the 17th century as you have already seen in previous chapters. Lindeström himself, in his book "Geographia Americae" tells us that the Dutch fort had four bastions and that his redesigned fort also had four bastions. The horizontal scale of the fort is clearly indicated on his elevation drawing. I took all my data and built an accurate digital model of a perfectly proportioned fort, on which the drawings to the right were based. I used the notion of a perfect fort because Lindeström's drawing seems extremely idealized. The view was then rotated from an aerial position downward and to the left, until I had created a realistically scaled front elevation.

The accurate frontal view I arrived at almost exactly matches the forms in the Lindeström drawing. The primary differences being that I am convinced that Lindeström intentionally exaggerated the heights of his fort rendition for presentation purposes. This is evident if the bar scale below the drawing is applied to the drawing vertically. Doing so would make the overall fort the impossibly absurd height of over 70 feet.

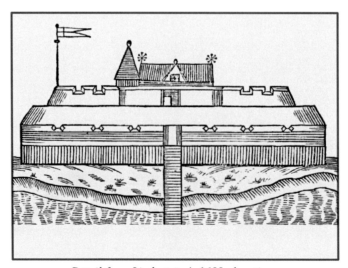

Detail from Lindeström's 1655 elevation.

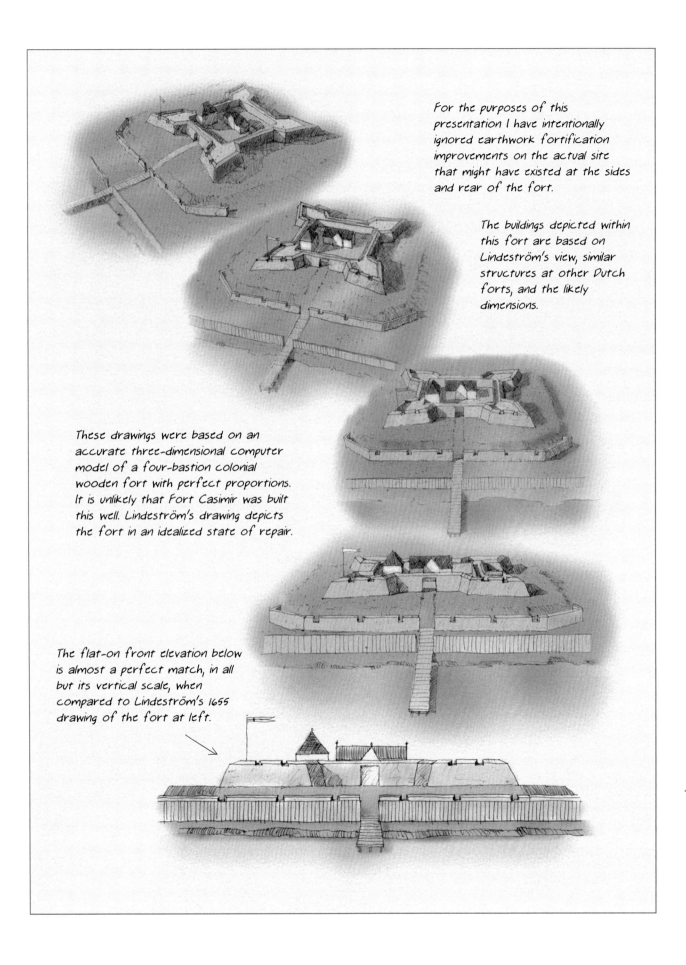

For the purposes of this presentation I have intentionally ignored earthwork fortification improvements on the actual site that might have existed at the sides and rear of the fort.

The buildings depicted within this fort are based on Lindeström's view, similar structures at other Dutch forts, and the likely dimensions.

These drawings were based on an accurate three-dimensional computer model of a four-bastion colonial wooden fort with perfect proportions. It is unlikely that Fort Casimir was built this well. Lindeström's drawing depicts the fort in an idealized state of repair.

The flat-on front elevation below is almost a perfect match, in all but its vertical scale, when compared to Lindeström's 1655 drawing of the fort at left.

Topography of the Fort Casimir Site
Assumptions from Historical Terrain Analysis

In 1986, Edward and Louise Heite where commissioned by the Trustees of the New Castle Commons to undertake an archeological investigation of the presumed site of Fort Casimir to determine what, if anything, remained underground. Their comprehensive findings are recorded in "Report of Phase I Archeological and Historical Investigations at the Site of Fort Casimir, New Castle, Delaware." In the excavation narrative, numerous examples of artifacts and soil stratification conditions are presented. Evidence of the fort's existence was clear; however it is not the kind of hard structural evidence to positively define the fort's construction and pinpoint its location. The Heite report is thorough and their desire to pursue further study is made clear.

For my purposes, the Heites provide an interesting compilation of topographical data pertaining to the site of the fort. Benjamin Henry Latrobe, famous for his landscape plan for the Capitol in Washington, DC, made a survey of New Castle in 1805. He accurately rendered profiles of the terrain. The Heites reinterpreted the Latrobe data into a contour map focusing on the immediate area they assumed to be the location of the fort. The Heites report also included a topographical map made in 1927 by Remington and Vosbury for the city of New Castle. This map reflects the general contours seen in the Latrobe profiles. It also clearly locates a large marsh area on the west side of Second Street. When the two maps are closely compared there is an unusual elevated area on the Latrobe/Heite map on Market Street and something quite similar in the same location on the Remington and Vosbury map, which refers to Market Street as Second Street. A structure approximately 200 feet square could have fit neatly on that raised plot of land.

In my conjectural site plan of Fort Casimir (bottom drawing opposite page) I have combined the data from both maps and plotted the likely location and scale of the fort. This is not conclusive evidence for the site of the fort. Only further study and professional archeological discoveries can achieve that, but it does provide a plausible possibility that can satisfy a number of critical criteria.

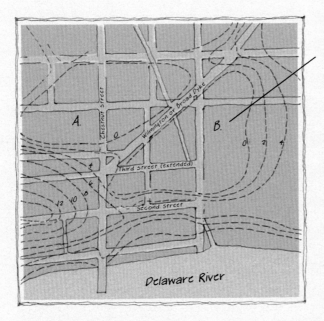

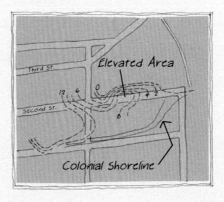

Areas A and B were at very low elevations and as a result were probably quite marshy.

This re-drawn contour map is based on Remington and Vosbury's "City of New Castle, Delaware, Sanitary System Index Map, 1927," as published in the Heites phase one archeological report.

This re-drawn partial contour map is based on a drawing by Edward and Louise Heite. Their original map was developed from Benjamin Latrobe's 1804 survey. The "Elevated Area" is particularly interesting.

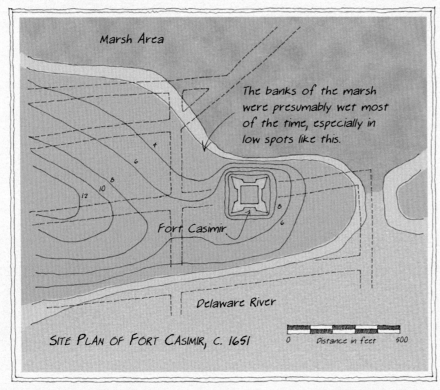

The banks of the marsh were presumably wet most of the time, especially in low spots like this.

SITE PLAN OF FORT CASIMIR, C. 1651

0   Distance in feet   500

The contour map to the left is a conjectural composite of both the maps above. Fort Casimir and the original shoreline were located using the topographical data from the above source material.

See pages 84-85 for comparative analysis.

The scale of this drawing is slightly larger than the drawings above.

Fort Casimir 1651 - 1654
A Basic Dutch Fort in Marshland

Fort Casimir was built in 1651, under the direction of the Director General of New Netherland, Petrus Stuyvesant. It was named after Ernst Casimir I, a respected Dutch count. The original Dutch fort, Fort Nassau, built on the west side of the Delaware River, near present-day Philadelphia, had been rendered useless by the more southern Swedish construction of Fort Christina. Dutch ships entering Delaware Bay had to pass Fort Christina to get to Fort Nassau. The new fort thereby reversed the roles of military river dominance back in favor of the Dutch.

Stuyvesant, already burdened with the security of Manhattan, had neither the money nor the manpower to properly build, maintain, or defend Fort Casimir. Perhaps it was doomed from the start simply because the site of its construction was so wet. The fort was built next to a swamp on a relatively low lying peninsula in an area called the Sandhook. The only thing it seemed to have going for it was relatively deep water access on the riverfront. Regardless of the location's obvious shortcomings, the wood and sod four-bastioned fort was erected and armed and, most importantly for Stuyvesant, flew the Dutch colors.

In 1654, a Swedish force under the command of the governor of New Sweden, Johan Risingh, took Fort Casimir. Both Risingh and Per Lindeström give detailed accounts of the capture. Lindeström states that the fort was taken on May 21, 1654. To honor that day, Trinity Sunday, the fort was renamed Fort Trinity. The fort contained twelve iron cannons and one brass three-pounder, all without gunpowder or ammunition. The defender's muskets were mostly broken. Risingh's journal states that the entire garrison was occupied by only nine soldiers and a Sergeant Gerrit Bicker who was the commandant. They did not resist.

The Swedes now once again controlled the Delaware River and had taken over a fort so badly decayed that it required rebuilding practically from the ground up. From the moment the fort's overhaul began, Stuyvesant's counter attack strategy was forming.

Fort Casimir, circa 1654, looking toward the marsh

Fort Casimir was built by the Dutch in 1651 on a point of land bordered on the north and west sides by a marsh and on the east by the Delaware River.

Note the "makelaar" roof ornaments.

Fort Casimir, like all the other wooden forts in 17th century North America, was in constant need of maintenance. Records tell us that the fort was undermanned during the early years of Dutch control. This may explain the description given by Per Lindeström in 1654, in which he states "....when we arrived in New Sweden, it [Fort Casimir] had fallen into almost total decay."

Makelaar

The curious ornamental features that can clearly be seen on the Linderström elevation are most likely traditional Dutch gable ornaments called "makelaar."

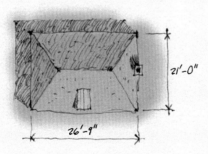

21'-0"

26'-9"

Roof plan of the courthouse building that stood in Fort Orange (Albany, NY).

Perhaps the hip-roofed courthouse building at Fort Orange was similiar to the pyramid-roofed structure depicted by Lindeström in Fort Casimir. This drawing of the Fort Orange courthouse was based on the research of Jaap Schipper, B.N.A., Amsterdam, 1985.

Fort Trinity (Trefaldighet in Swedish)
May 21, 1654 - August 30, 1655

Four hundred sixty-six days—Fort Trinity's lifespan was very short. On Trinity Sunday, May 21, 1654 (Julian calendar), Governor Johan Risingh enraged Petrus Stuyvesant when he captured the under-manned and poorly maintained Fort Casimir. It was Risingh's decision and his alone. He could have left the decaying fort since, in its dilapidated condition, it presented little threat to New Sweden. The Governor's reasoning was that Stuyvesant would eventually restore Fort Casimir and completely undermine New Sweden's investments in the Delaware region by cutting off their access to the Atlantic.

Risingh committed men and resources to upgrade the fort. Lindeström did the engineering and Captain Sven Skute was placed in charge of the work to see that it was carried out. Skute also served as Fort Trinity's commander. The fort was initially armed with four cannons, twelve-pounders taken from the ship, "Eagle," which had transported Risingh and Lindeström to New Sweden.

Lindeström's plans called for the repair and upgrading of the bastions, the construction of fortified trenches, and the erection of a palisade along the river bank. Skute and twenty men worked all through the summer of 1654, building the palisade only to have it badly damaged on October 24, 1654, by a terrible storm. It is unlikely that much of the Lindeström plan, depicted in his elevation, was ever completed. There simply wasn't enough time, money, or men. This seems to be borne out in Dutch records after they regained the fort.

Stuyvesant commanded over three hundred men and a fleet of seven ships, which included the leased 36-gun warship *de Waegh*. On August 30, 1655, Captain Skute allowed the Dutch force to sail slightly past Fort Trinity and anchor on its weakest side. This was a tactical blunder. The Dutch negotiated with Skute and at the same time began digging siege trenches from which they could easily bombard the Swedes. Skute surrendered. A few days later Stuyvesant sailed five miles north and attacked Fort Christina. Risingh was defeated and forced to give up not only the fort, but all of New Sweden.

1. At the time of the Swedish capture in May of 1654, Lindeström states that there are twenty-one houses at Sandhook. Tobacco was grown with varying degrees of success. Other crops included barley, corn, hops, beans, squash, and other fruits and vegetables.

2. The fort that was the primary focus of repairs. Lindeström's elevation suggests that parapets with embrasures may have been added to the bastions.

3. The exact length of the main dock is not known. It would have been extended far enough into the Delaware River to accommodate large ships. Probably a bit farther than I have depicted here.

4. The badly damaged palisade was probably incomplete in August of 1655, when the Dutch capture took place.

5. The Lindeström elevation indicates the construction of earthwork fortifications. They were probably wood and sod walls similar to the parapets of the bastions, standing in front of a 4 or 5 foot trench. Embrasures for cannon are clearly visible on the Lindeström drawing.

6. The marsh.

7. The land north of the fort was low and wet. The Swedes may have assumed that if attacking ships could be stopped before they passed the fort this land would provide some protection.

New Amstel 1657 - 1664
The Fort and the Community

Petrus Stuyvesant was indebted to the city of Amsterdam for leasing their 36-gun ship *de Waegh*. As payment, the Dutch West India Company negotiated a deal in which Amsterdam, in exchange for their services, accepted ownership of a portion of the land on the west side of the Delaware River. Thus began the colony of New Amstel – a colony within a colony.

Life in the colony was a struggle. Sickness was common in New Amstel/Sandhook. The swamps that adjoined the settlement were a breeding ground for mosquitoes, flies, rats, and all manner of disease bearing creatures. That, combined with the limited access to even the remotest form of effective medicine, brought about a constant state of disease and death. In June of 1658, Jacob Alrichs wrote a letter to Petrus Stuyvesant describing a terrible fever that was raging in New Amstel. The labor force of freemen and slaves was reduced to such an extent that very few were still able to work. Under

A view of Fort Casimir, circa 1656, from the main throughfare. In present-day New Castle this would be Second Street.

such a burden the survival of the colony at times seemed doomed to failure. Throughout the early colonial period both the Swedes and the Dutch recorded accounts such as this.

Both skilled and unskilled slaves supplemented New Amstel's workforce. The white population of Delaware was approximately five hundred persons by 1664. It is estimated that in addition to that number there were less than fifty African slaves in all of Delaware. The number of slaves at Sandhook would have been considerably less.

For the mostly Protestant residents of New Amstel, religion was part of everyday life. The written records consistently reflect the general devoutness of the community. Prayers are constantly offered seeking divine intervention in the resolution of daily hardships. It is therefore interesting to note that, unlike Rensselaerswijck and Manhattan, no church was ever built in the Dutch colony of New Amstel. Services were conducted in the court building inside Fort Casimir.

Farms were located both northeast and southwest of Fort Casimir. Wheat, barley, rye, and corn were staples in New Amstel and in other parts of New Netherland. In addition to grain, fruits and vegetables were also grown. Of all the foods that made up the diet of the settlement in New Amstel there was one treat that everyone enjoyed: watermelon. Per Lindeström writes "…this has an exceedingly delicious and beautiful taste and immediately melts in the mouth. These watermelons are used to eat and drink during the hot summer, as they refresh and cool off a person strongly."

Meat was provided by domestic livestock and wild game. Transporting livestock was done by sea and land. In both the Swedish and Dutch periods there is frequent mention of a particular vessel that is used to carry livestock and goods to and from the colony. It is not clear if it is the same ship, but it is definitely the same type of ship, a galliot. This versatile eight to fifteen ton, fore and aft rigged ship was capable of carrying a wide variety of cargoes. The drawing on page 45 shows how the galliot could be used to carry lumber and bricks from Fort Orange. Galliot trips to and from Manhattan and Virginia were also quite commonly noted.

Although some livestock was transported by sea, most were driven overland in much the same manner depicted in countless western movies. One cattle drive, which originated in Heemstede, near Manhattan, contained over forty head of cattle which included twenty cows, ten calves, one bull, and approximately sixteen oxen. One can only imagine the hardships faced along the way considering the animals' condition upon arrival in New Amstel. In another of the many letters from Alrichs to Stuyvesant the cattle are described as in poor condition and mostly lame. He goes on to state that many were slaughtered since they were not expected to survive.

Colonial life was difficult and fraught with danger. Survival was in no way assured. Keeping the population healthy and supplying food and shelter were essential if Stuyvesant's plan to strengthen and develop New Amstel were ever to succeed. In 1655, he appointed Jean Paul Jacquet as Vice-Director and placed him in charge of its organization, governance, and planning.

In actuality the planning of the community had begun before Jacquet's time. In 1652, Peter Lourensen had received a lot approximately sixty feet wide and three hundred feet deep. The depth of this lot is interesting to note when compared with a present day map of New Castle. Three hundred feet is nearly the same measurement as the distance between Second and Third Streets.

The security of Fort Casimir was of paramount importance to Vice-Director Jacquet. He therefore decreed that no building be erected in the immediate areas north, east, and west of the fort. Jacquet wanted a concentrated community to develop to the south. In 1655 he ordered that lots forty to fifty feet wide and one hundred feet deep be set along a new street, located behind

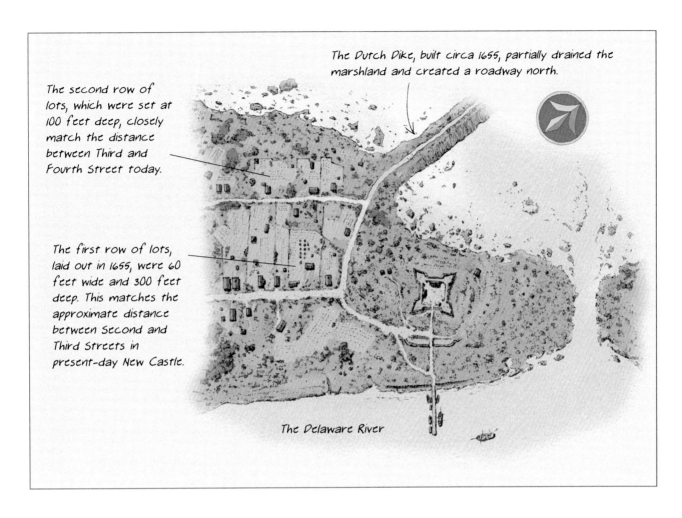

The Dutch Dike, built circa 1655, partially drained the marshland and created a roadway north.

The second row of lots, which were set at 100 feet deep, closely match the distance between Third and Fourth Street today.

The first row of lots, laid out in 1655, were 60 feet wide and 300 feet deep. This matches the approximate distance between Second and Third Streets in present-day New Castle.

The Delaware River

the houses which already existed on Lourensen's block. One hundred feet matches almost exactly the distance between Third and Fourth Streets today. Comparing the lot arrangements of 1652 and 1655 with the same area of today's New Castle, it is quite clear that the original Dutch footprint is still very apparent.

From the very beginning Jacquet had declared Fort Casimir a ruin that would need to be rebuilt from the ground up. Among all the improvements that Jacquet initiated and implemented in the community, he failed completely in renovating the fort. In the end the Dutch had achieved little more than the Swedes in putting the fort into combat-ready condition. Fort Casimir, like Fort Orange in Albany and Fort New Amsterdam in Manhattan, were ill prepared for the eventual doomsday that was coming.

The map above indicates the improvements made by the Dutch in the later years of their control. Most of these features are apparent today in this area of New Castle.

The English Attack
September 30, 1664

The director who presided over the colony of New Amstel was Alexander D'Hinoyossa, a veteran of the Dutch West India Company's wars to conquer Brazil. Considered by some to be a harsh ruler, D'Hinoyossa had been successfully carrying on business with the English in Maryland with much of the profits winding up in his pocket. He was comfortable and New Amstel's future seemed bright. All this was about to change.

In 1664, England took New Netherland. Naval and land forces under the command of Colonel Richard Nicholls, were dispatched by the Duke of York who claimed the land by the authority of the king. In Manhattan, Petrus Stuyvesant, facing overwhelming odds, accepted the English terms of surrender. Fort Orange fell a few days later. Nicholls sent Sir Robert Carr with two ships the 36-gun *Guinea* and the 10-gun *William and Nicholas,* along with more than one hundred thirty soldiers, to take Fort Casimir (renamed at that time Fort New Amstel).

On September 30, 1664, Carr's flotilla sailed within range of Fort Casimir. D'Hinoyossa, believing that he had the support of the local population and his English friends in Maryland, had rejected Carr's terms of surrender. The orders were given and devastating salvos from the two warships splintered the riverfront walls of the fort. Returning fire from the fort's cannons had little effect. At the time of the attack, Fort Casimir's garrison consisted of thirty men. With their attention fixed on manning the guns against the ships' broadsides, they were unable to prevent one hundred thirty English troops from attacking the fort from the rear. With shrapnel flying, and under relentless musket fire, one third of the Dutch defenders were killed and wounded. Under hopeless conditions Fort Casimir capitulated. After the battle, English soldiers plundered the fort and the entire Delaware Valley. Carr took the best for himself, seizing D'Hinoyossa's land and property.

The fall of the Dutch fortifications along the Delaware River brought to an end the glory days of New Netherland. For a brief period of one year and two months in 1673, Dutch forces under the command of Admiral Cornelius Evertsen re-took New Netherland. Although Dutch rule was reinstated, government support for the restored colony was weak at best. In the end New Netherland was returned to the English as part of a treaty agreement.

After Fort Casimir
Influences of the Past

Fort Casimir is long gone. The cannonballs that shattered its bastions have settled deep in the dust of history. Looking back what can be learned from its existence?

As a fort, Casimir failed every time it was challenged. In 1654, the Dutch surrendered to the Swedes. In 1655, the Swedes surrendered to the Dutch. In 1664, the Dutch surrendered to the English. In 1673, the English surrendered to the Dutch, and in 1674, the English took it back again. Actually, Fort Orange in Albany, Fort Good Hope near Hartford, and Fort Amsterdam in Manhattan all fell well short of their defensive intent. This curious commonality can be explained by making a simple analogy. Forts are like the locks placed on boxes. The greater the perceived value of the contents the better the lock. The Dutch stone forts of Asia are still standing, as are many of the massive fortifications of 17th century Europe, while the North American installations have long since rotted away. In the final analysis, it all came down to the fact that guarding a box full of corn, beans, tobacco, and a few beaver pelts could not compare with the riches of the Orient or securing one's own country. Military priorities were placed where they provided the greatest advantage. In the case of the North American forts, the structures themselves seemed to state dominion not power, providing protection from Indian warfare, but little resistance against a full scale European-style assault.

For the colonists, it seemed to matter little who was in charge as long as their lives could continue with as little hardship as possible. Fort Casimir failed, but the little settlement of Sandhook that evolved into a Swedish town and then into the larger community of New Amstel and finally New Castle, survived and flourished. This recurrent pattern of social stability over political domination seems to be a constant in human behavior and one that can be seen in all corners of the globe.

The impact of history is in the influence it has on daily life. The 17th century presence of the Dutch in New Netherland and the Swedish/Dutch mix in the Delaware region can still be felt to this day. It runs much deeper than place names and facts in history books. It is embedded in the lifestyle of all who live and work in the region. It is an unconscious and hidden response to the past. It may manifest itself in the phrasing of a question, general business practices, or a certain lack of formality in social situations, barely perceptible at first perhaps, but it is there, a subtle reminder of the culture that once defined New Netherland.

Arnoldus de la Grange built a windmill, circa 1681,
on the inland side of the ruins of Fort Casimir.

A Mountain of Gold

Of all the stories connected with the colony and Fort Casimir the most bizarre and interesting was recorded by Per Lindeström in his "Geographia Americae, pages 162-163." The story is about an encounter between the Swedish governor, Johan Printz, and a Rennapi Indian. Printz had shown this Indian a gold bracelet and asked if the Indian had any knowledge of such a substance. The Indian said he knew of a mountain were this same material could be taken from the ground. Printz wanted proof. After some time the Indian returned with a chunk of gold-bearing rock, the size of two fists. The gold was examined and found to be of good quality. The gold extracted from the rock was made into rings and bracelets. The Indian placed little value on the gold and Printz had been able to trade a few pieces of cloth for it. The greedy governor wanted more. When the Indian returned to his people and boasted of how he had obtained the cloth the chief was furious. Fearing that disclosure of the "mountain of gold" would bring ruin to his people, he ordered the Indian killed. The existence of the mountain has remained a mystery ever since.

4.

Comparisons

New discoveries are what make the study of
historical places and events so exciting and it
is from that data that future historians and
artists will build more convincing theories.

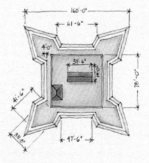

1905 Cooper Drawing of Fort Casimir

Comparing Documentary Drawings

Historical information can, and often, accumulates over time. Comparing the illustration made in 1905 for Alexander Cooper's book on Fort Casimir with my 2011 drawing of the same fort, reflects the vastly different conclusions that can arise from an improved research base. It is doubtful that Cooper considered the European tradition from which any North American fort in the early colonial period would have evolved. I have spent 20 years studying the wooden forts built by the Dutch in New York State. I am an architect and historical artist deeply interested in how buildings fit together. The motivation driving my approach to Fort Casimir is entirely different than that of Mr. Cooper.

Among the many divergent points between the two drawings is the interpretation of the stockade. The Cooper drawing depicts the fort atop a raised, geometrically perfect platform tightly surrounded by an enclosed fence of vertical boards. Historical records indicate that the stockade was linear in design and built along the riverbank. Cooper places the fort very near the river's edge. The Heite study locates the high ground of the site centered about three hundred and thirty feet from the shoreline. The site

2011 Tantillo Drawing of Fort Casimir

topography alone makes a compelling argument for the fort's actual location away from the river and much closer to the marsh.

The Cooper drawing is a very literal translation of the Lindeström elevation. In rigidly sticking to that premise the buildings within the fort reflect little in the way of

colonial architectural features. The wharf is completely without precedent. The dock is ramped downward into the river (page 60), a disastrous situation considering the loading of barrels onto ships. The two drawings presented here are separated by one hundred and six years of accumulating historical data. Side by side they could hardly be more dissimilar.

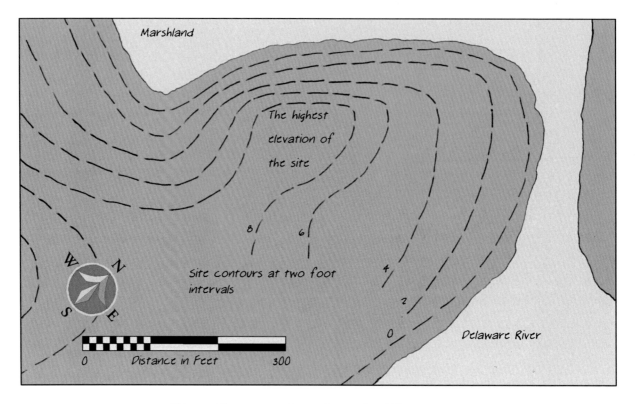

Heite Contours from Latrobe Elevations

Relationship of Fort Casimir to the Site

There is evidence that strongly suggests the specific location of Fort Casimir. It can be derived from an interpretation of the stepped terrain feature depicted in Edward and Louise Heites' archeological study of 1986, as seen on page 67. When I studied the configuration of contour lines on the drawing, the squared "high ground feature" struck me as man-made and intentional. What's more, when a four-bastioned fort scaled from Per Lindeström's 1655 drawing is positioned on the Heites' site feature, it fits almost perfectly. Coincidence perhaps, but intriguing none the less. In and of itself this is not definitive proof but it is certainly hard to ignore.

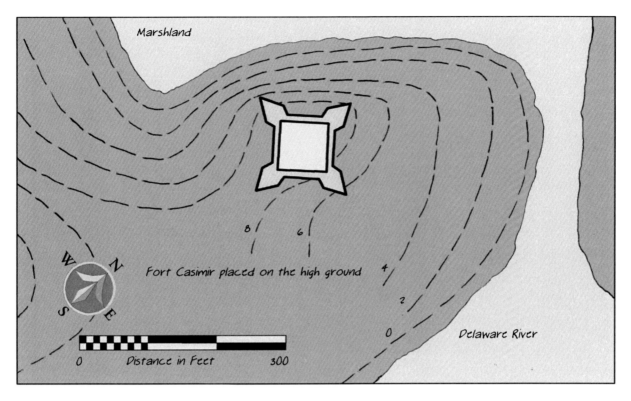

Marshland

Fort Casimir placed on the high ground

8   6   4   2   0

Delaware River

Distance in Feet

0   300

Fort Casimir on High Ground Site Feature

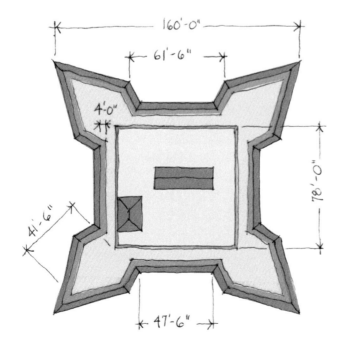

160'-0"

61'-6"

4'-0"

78'-0"

41'-6"

47'-6"

A four-bastion fort of approximately this size fits well on the "high ground" site feature depicted on the Heites' 1986 topographical contour map.

The dimensions of this fort design are based on the 1655 drawing of Fort Casimir/Trinity by Per Lindeström.

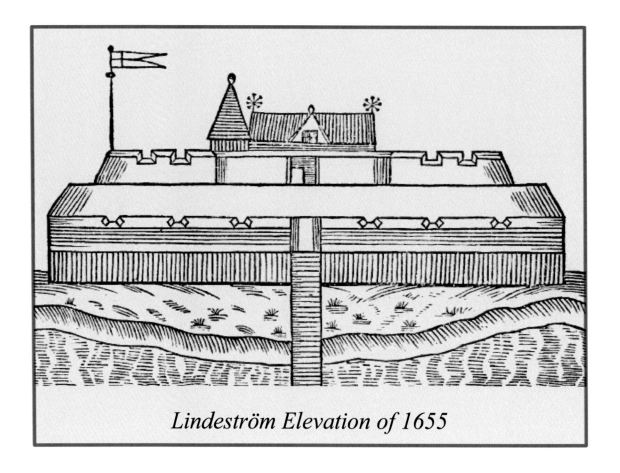

Lindeström Elevation of 1655

Comparing the Elevations

Initially I thought that the 1655 Lindeström's drawing was pure fiction. That it represented what he wished the fort was, not what it was in reality. The fort as drawn seemed rooted in an idealized notion of medieval fortifications and castles. That was my first impression anyway. Then I began to wonder why he would make something like that up. So if it wasn't whimsical what did it mean? The answer came after building an accurate digital model of a four-bastion fort in my computer. The dimensions I used were based on Lindeström's scale. I placed my fort on an elevated plane as suggested by the Heite survey and included an outer fortified earthwork. When the model was complete and I rotated it to a full-on front elevation, I was astonished to see the remarkable resemblance it had to Lindeström's drawing. It matched well enough to solve the mystery for me.

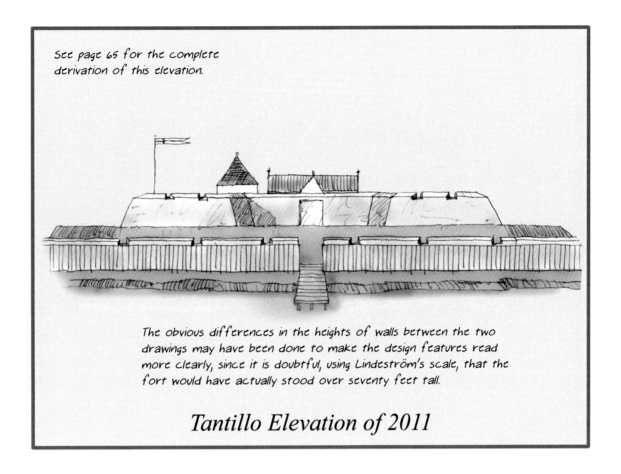

See page 65 for the complete derivation of this elevation.

The obvious differences in the heights of walls between the two drawings may have been done to make the design features read more clearly, since it is doubtful, using Lindeström's scale, that the fort would have actually stood over seventy feet tall.

Tantillo Elevation of 2011

In time others may find new information that will completely void this and the other conclusions expressed in this book. I accept that possibility with the knowledge that my work is just as susceptible to error as my talented predecessors. New discoveries are what make the study of historical places and events so exciting and it is from that data that future historians and artists will build more convincing theories.

FLAGS OVER NEW CASTLE, DELAWARE

In Chronological Order (1624 - 1777)

The Dutch State Flag

Dutch build the first fort on the Delaware River. *(Orange stripe to c.1630)*

1624

Union Jack of Great Britian

Sir Robert Carr captures Fort Casimir

1664

Flag of the Dutch West India Company

Petrus Stuyvesant builds Fort Casimir at Sandhook

1651

Flag of the Dutch West India Company

Admiral Cornelius Evertsen retakes Fort Casimir

1673

State Flag of Sweden

Johan Risingh captures Fort Casimir and renames it Fort Trinity

1654

Union Jack of Great Britian

Treaty of Westminster returns Delaware to British rule

1674

Flag of the Dutch West India Company

Petrus Stuyvesant retakes Fort Trinity and renames it Fort New Amstel

1655

Grand Union Flag

Early years of the American Revolution, preferred flag of George Washington

1775

Flag of the City of Amsterdam

Amsterdam is given all the land on the west side of the Delaware River.

1657

First Official Flag of the United States of America

First star represented the state of Delaware

1777

Note: Delaware was administered by the province of New York until 1683 and the arrival of William Penn.

Final Observations
Picturing History
by Peter A. Douglas

In this book's text and vivid illustrations we have seen in detail how Fort Casimir rose from the humid and inhospitable wilderness through the sheer strength and sweat of men more at home on the temperate shores of the North Sea. We have seen Len's images of this vanished fort rising from the surrounding marsh, huge balks of buried timber, plank upon mossy plank, to form the massive bastions and walls to contain and retain the many tons of dirt and fill. Briefly come to life for us, we have caught sight of the broad gun platforms, the magazines and storehouses, and the barracks that were home of a kind to the luckless garrison. And we have seen how the fort changed hands back and forth between the Dutch and the Swedes before succumbing, as so many have, to English cannonballs and musket fire.

Len has said, "I am interested in picturing history, and I try to base it on evidence that I feel very confident in." This confidence grew as Len burrowed for months into the story of Casimir. Ultimately, in his computer the electronic skeleton of the fort was fleshed out, the bones growing and acquiring musculature. From contemporary sketches and accounts the stronghold took form and life again, showing us how the Dutch planted their tricolor in the Delaware muck and took tenure of that untamed land. It was, though, a land that threatened and inevitably took back this bold human intrusion; the fort grew from the landscape and the landscape would reclaim it.

In thus "picturing history," Len is basing his theories and images not on his free imagination but on this vital imagination guided by the facts that he feels are authentic and of which he is convinced. He is quick to admit that any representation of the world of centuries past must derive from a certain amount of speculation, and he's the first to say, "I could be totally wrong." I demurred and assured him that few people have poked around Fort Casimir as much as he has, and such modesty is misplaced. For Len it is not speculation, but what I prefer to call "speculative information," unearthing of the details of bygone times through extensive research and informed deduction to produce the best conclusion.

So we have witnessed the birth and the death of Fort Casimir, and the brief span of its existence that separated these two events, a mere thirteen years. In his preface Len stated that this fort fascinates him because it is unremarkable and typical of its time and place. We have caught some glimpses of its unremarkable story, a passing appearance, one small point of color in the broad tableau of New Netherland. Len has always aimed in his historical sketches and paintings to capture "the texture of time," and here I believe we have a richly woven cloth. True, the part played by Casimir in the huge picture of New Netherland and its fur trade and international rivalries was slim and obscure, and it was far from a success as an impregnable fortress. It had, nevertheless, its own moment in history, and we must remember that what's important is not the battle won but the battle waged.

Acknowledgments

There are many complicated steps in writing and illustrating a book of this type. Its credibility depends on the commitment of the author to accurately represent the facts. In the case of 17th century New Netherland much of what an artist depicts involves informed guesses and speculation because only partial historic documentation exists. Without the help of talented historians I would not know where to begin. I would like to thank Charles T. Gehring, the New Netherland Institute, and the New Netherland Research Center for providing me with the opportunity and the knowledge base, without which this work would never have been possible. Charly has been my friend and inspiration for a long time. His work in meticulously translating the surviving Dutch documents of that long ago time are an invaluable contribution to American culture.

I would also like to thank a great archeologist, Paul Huey, for his help and support over the years. Paul's early work on Fort Orange in Albany piqued my interest and inspired many paintings and drawings of that subject over the last twenty five years. Paul's research has influenced much of my thinking about Fort Casimir as well. I also wish to thank Edward and Louise Heite for their comprehensive archeological report. I referred to it constantly and it lead me to a greater understanding and appreciation of the fort site and its setting in New Castle.

The fact that this book exists at all is largely due to the encouragement of Marilyn Douglas. I wish to thank her for convincing me to do this project. Her husband, Peter Douglas, provided me with much needed support and encouragement. His suggestions helped shape the book and his interesting accounts of the progress of the project interspersed through the book add immensely to the story of Fort Casimir. For his patience and contributions I am sincerely grateful.

I would like to thank Bill Greer and Jim Sefcik for bearing with me during the business phase of this work. It isn't always easy to work with an artist who keeps changing his mind.

It seems like such a cliché for an author to thank his or her spouse. The truth of the matter is that without Corliss I would be nowhere. I cannot begin to express my thanks to her for a lifetime of support. So to keep it manageable, thanks, Cor, for taking the time to patiently edit this work. Your contributions were the most helpful.

I would also like to thank Celina Nehme for the inspiration she provided in helping me develop the illustration technique for the book.

Finally, I would like to thank Per Lindeström for his incredible documentary record of New Sweden. Through his eyes we have the precious opportunity to see the past, experience daily life in colonial America and appreciate the courage and energy it took to build a nation.

Bibliography

Bradley, J. W. *Before Albany: An Archaeology of Native-Dutch Relations in the Capital Region 1600-1664*, New York State Museum, Albany 2007

Dahlgren, S. and Norman, H. *The Rise and Fall of New Sweden*, Bohuslaningens Boktryckeri 1988

Duffy, C. *Fire & Stone - The Science of Fortress Warfare 1660-1860*, Peters Fraser & Dunlop, London 1975

Gehring, C. T. *New York Historical Manuscripts: Dutch, Volumes XVIII-XIX, Delaware Papers (Dutch Period)*, Genealogical Publishing Co., Inc., Baltimore, MD 1981

Griffith, P. *The Vauban Fortifications of France*, Osprey Publishing, Oxford, 2006

Heite and Heite, *Report of Phase One Archeological and Historical Investigations at the Site of Fort Casimir, New Castle, Delaware* 1986

Holm, Thomas Campanius *Kort beskrifning om provincien Nya Swerige uti America: som nu fortjden af the Engelske kallas*, J. H. Werner 1702

Lindeström, P. *Geographia Americae with An Account of the Delaware Indians*, Arno Press, New York 1979

Munroe, J. A. *Colonial Delaware a History*, Millwood New York, KTO Press 1978

O'Callaghan, E. B. *History of New Netherland or New York under the Dutch, Volume I*, D. Appleton and Company, New York 1855

Shomette, D. G. and Haslach R. D. *Raid on America; The Dutch Naval Campaign of 1672-1674*, University of South Carolina Press 1988

Shorto, R. *The Island at the Center of the World*, Doubleday, New York, London, Toronto, Sidney, Auckland 2004

Stallcup, L. S. *Steelcoat: Stalcop genealogy and New Sweden* www.stalcopfamily.com

Van den Bogaert, H. M. *A Journey into Mohawk and Oneida Country, 1634-1635*, translated and edited by Charles T. Gehring and William A. Starna, Syracuse University Press 1988

Van der Donck, A. *A Description of New Netherland*, edited by Charles T. Gehring and William A. Starna, Translated by Diederik Willem Goedhuys, University of Nebraska Press 2008

Van Laer, A. J. F. *Minutes of the Court of Rensselaerswyck 1648-1652*, Albany The University of the State of New York 1922

Venema, J. *Beverwijck: A Dutch Village on the American Frontier, 1652-1664*, Verloren/Hilversum, The Netherlands, State University of New York Press 2003

Wilson, T. *Flags at Sea*, Naval Institute Press, Maryland 1999

The New Netherland Institute

The New Netherland Institute (NNI) is an independent, non-profit, non-state organization providing support for the New Netherland Research Center (NNRC) and NNI programs through fundraising and other activities that tell the story of the Dutch colonial history of America. Created in 1986 as the Friends of the New Netherland Project, the NNI provides significant financial assistance to transcribe, translate, and publish the early Dutch colonial records and documents in the collections of the New York State Library and the State Archives. These materials constitute the world's largest collection of original documentation of the Dutch West India Company and the New World colonies. They provide insight into the continuing impact of the early Dutch culture, language, and law on America.

Opened to the public in November 2010, the NNRC is located in the New York State Research Library. It provides a permanent location where students, educators, scholars, and researchers worldwide can have access to translations of early Dutch colonial manuscripts and a vast library of early documents, books, and reference works that tell the fascinating story of the Dutch global reach during the American colonial period and its lasting impact on today's world.

The NNRC continues the work of the New Netherland Project (NNP). Founded in 1974 to translate and publish the original 17th-century Dutch documents of New Netherland, the NNP is one of the most ambitious translation projects ever conceived. With more than 7,000 pages translated to date, the NNP has produced groundbreaking insight into the colony of New Netherland and the Dutch in colonial America. The work of the NNP gained international acclaim as the inspiration and foundation of Russell Shorto's 2004 best seller, *The Island at the Center of the World*. Through the NNRC, work begun by the NNP is being expanded to encompass materials in collections around the globe.

Made in the USA
San Bernardino, CA
14 June 2017